Priorities *in* Practice

The Essentials of Social Studies, Grades K–8

Priorities *in* Practice

The Essentials of Social Studies, Grades K–8

Effective Curriculum, Instruction, and Assessment

Kathy Checkley

Association for Supervision and Curriculum Development
Alexandria, Virginia USA

Association for Supervision and Curriculum Development
1703 N. Beauregard St. • Alexandria, VA 22311-1714 USA
Phone: 800-933-2723 or 703-578-9600 • Fax: 703-575-5400
Web site: www.ascd.org • E-mail: member@ascd.org
Author guidelines: www.ascd.org/write

About the Author: Kathy Checkley has been a journalist for more than 25 years and has spent the past 14 years focusing on issues in education.

Gene R. Carter, *Executive Director;* Nancy Modrak, *Publisher;* Julie Houtz, *Director of Book Editing & Production;* Miriam Goldstein, *Project Manager;* Georgia Park, *Senior Graphic Designer;* Circle Graphics, *Typesetter;* Sarah Plumb, *Production Specialist*

All Web links in this book are correct as of the publication date below but may have become inactive or otherwise modified since that time. If you notice a deactivated or changed link, please e-mail books@ascd. org with the words "Link Update" in the subject line. In your message, please specify the Web link, the book title, and the page number on which the link appears.

PAPERBACK ISBN-13: 978-1-4166-0645-1   ASCD product #107099   s1/08
Also available as an e-book through ebrary, netLibrary, and many online booksellers (see Books in Print for the ISBNs).

Quantity discounts for the paperback edition only: 10–49 copies, 10%; 50+ copies, 15%; for 1,000 or more copies, call 800-933-2723, ext. 5634, or 703-575-5634. For desk copies: member@ascd.org.

Library of Congress Cataloging-in-Publication Data

Checkley, Kathy.
   The essentials of social studies, grades K-8 : effective curriculum,
instruction, and assessment / Kathy Checkley.
        p. cm. — (Priorities in practice)
   Includes bibliographical references and index.
   ISBN 978-1-4166-0645-1 (pbk. : alk. paper) 1. Social sciences—
Study and teaching (Elementary) 2. Social sciences—Study and teaching
(Middle school) I. Title.
   LB1584.C485 2008
   372.83—dc22

                                                      2007037814

17 16 15 14 13 12 11 10 09 08   1 2 3 4 5 6 7 8 9 10 11 12

PRIORITIES *in* PRACTICE

The Essentials of Social Studies, Grades K–8

Acknowledgments

Many thanks! This book could not have been written without the kindness, patience, and generosity of all the teachers and educators interviewed.

Special thanks go to Mary McFarland, for always being willing to clarify my thinking and provide resources to enhance my learning; to Susan Griffin, who always took time to point me in the right direction; to Jeff Passe and Peggy Altoff, for their candor and passion for social studies; and to Annenberg Media and the National Council for the Social Studies for producing such a fine series of professional development programs about social studies.

At the time this book was being written, educators interviewed could be reached at the following locations:

- Peggy Altoff, District 11, Colorado Springs, Colorado
- Betsy Bratek, Greenbelt Middle School, Greenbelt, Maryland
- Christina Doepel, G. James Gholson Middle School, Landover, Maryland
- Gale Ekiss, Arizona Geographic Alliance, Arizona State University, Tempe, Arizona
- Mary Knightly, Kensington Elementary School, Kensington, New Hampshire
- Kara Libby, Prince George's County Public Schools, Maryland
- Mary McFarland, education consultant, Chesterfield, Missouri
- Margit E. McGuire, Seattle University, Seattle, Washington
- Eileen Mesmer, Saltonstall School, Salem, Massachusetts
- Jeff Passe, University of North Carolina, Charlotte, North Carolina

• Osvaldo Rubio, Sherman Oaks Community Charter School, San Jose, California
• Jamie Sawatzky, Rocky Run Middle School, Chantilly, Virginia
• Elizabeth Sinclair, The New School, Seattle, Washington
• Mark J. Stout, Howard County Public School System, Maryland
• Kathleen Waffle, John F. Kennedy Elementary School, Newark, California
• Joann Winkler, Liberty Elementary School, Port Charlotte, Florida
• Roger D. Wolff, University of South Dakota, Vermillion, South Dakota
• Justin Zimmerman, North East Middle School, North East, Maryland

Finally, a special dedication to Tom Hoerr: you've been an inspiration to my family and so many others. This book is for you.

Preface

The business of public education in America is, and should be, to teach young people how to take charge of their own learning and to become responsible, informed, and engaged citizens.

—*Restoring the Balance Between Academics and Civic Engagement in Public Schools,* American Youth Policy Forum (2005)

It is the job of schools to ensure that students develop the qualities and skills that will enable them to contribute meaningfully to the needs of future societies. In the U.S. education field's current climate of accountability, however, this essential goal seems to be overlooked in favor of test preparation.

On her darkest days, a veteran educator admits, she believes that excluding social studies from the curriculum is part of a grand scheme to keep power in the hands of a controlling few. Think about it, she says: it stands to reason that if students aren't educated in democratic processes, they won't truly understand the need to get out and vote during an election—ensuring that those in elected office *stay* in elected office. She then observes that when "large groups of people become disenfranchised, things don't go well for those societies" and warns that the United States is going to be "sunk as a nation" if social studies continues to get short shrift in schools. Still, she hopes that as more educators and policymakers become aware of the damage caused by narrowing the curriculum, they will lobby for social studies to be restored to the learning program.

In this book, you'll find a number of educators who are equally dismayed to find that when forced to choose between delivering a broad liberal arts curriculum and boosting students' achievement on tests, a majority of school leaders will pick the latter. Yet plenty of teachers are overcoming the constraints of the current focus on testing. Innovative educators can find ways to ensure that their students will be able to hone the skills they need to actively participate in a democratic and global society.

Readers of this book will learn more about

• The challenges that elementary and middle school teachers face in keeping social studies in the curriculum.

• How to align social studies lessons with curriculum standards.

• Ways to promote students' deep understanding of social studies content.

• Why lessons and assessments should give students opportunities to solve problems, work on projects, and engage in simulations.

• How social studies can prepare students for a lifetime of active civic involvement.

• The kinds of professional development experiences that will help teachers bring the social studies curriculum to life in the classroom.

We suggest that you keep a pad of sticky notes close by as you read this book. We're certain that you'll find plenty of ideas for lesson planning, instruction, assessment, and professional development that you'll want to refer to again and again.

Trends in Social
Studies Education

Education, then, beyond all other devices of human origin,
is the great equalizer of the conditions of men—the balance-
wheel of the social machinery.

—Horace Mann

Fear can be a powerful motivator. Horace Mann, known as the father of public education in the United States, feared that uneducated immigrants, ignorant of their rights and obligations, would fail to support the democratic society to which they flocked. But, he reasoned, a common and free education could be the key to protecting the homeland from such an outcome. He argued that "every wise, humane measure adopted for [the immigrants'] welfare, directly promotes our own security" and observed that "the children of this people will soon possess the rights of men, whether they possess the characters of men or not" (Eakin, 2000). In addition to being the father of public education, then, Mann is the father of civic education: certain that schools could teach future citizens the values essential to democracy and citizenship.

There are few who would dispute Mann's assertion. But a new sort of fear has gripped many a modern educator: that of failing to meet accountability measures established by the No Child Left Behind Act (NCLB).

NCLB requires U.S. public schools to test 3rd–8th grade students in reading and math each year. Those schools that fail to bring enough of their students to proficiency in these subjects face escalating sanctions, including the establishment of a new curriculum, the replacement of school staff, and a decrease in managerial authority at the school. A school labeled "in need of improvement" for five consecutive years, risks being restructured or taken over by the state (Guilfoyle, 2006). Schools' fear of failure has resulted in a strong emphasis on math and reading instruction, particularly in elementary and middle schools, to the exclusion of nontested subjects. Among the disciplines receiving short shrift is social studies.

Horace Mann is turning over in his grave.

Accountability Run Amok: "Our Hands Are Tied"

Mary Knightly has her own worries. This award-winning, veteran teacher of 35 years once enthusiastically taught social studies to elementary school students of varied ages. But now, to her regret, she can no longer devote as much time to the subject. "I fear for social studies education," says Knightly, a 4th grade teacher at Kensington Elementary School in Kensington, New Hampshire. "What's happened in our school is happening in many. I have talked to my fellow teachers. They're teaching, at the most, two hours of social studies and science a week. I'm teaching three periods a week." With such a dramatic reduction in time, she says, students can't build a foundational knowledge of the subjects. "It's not a healthy balance," says Knightly. "I feel almost guilty sending students on who don't have a background in science and social studies."

Knightly isn't alone. In this era of accountability, many teachers report feeling frustrated and powerless to fight decisions made about curriculum and instruction. Results of a study of 376 elementary and secondary teachers in New Jersey, for example, showed that teachers "tended to teach to the test, often neglected individual students' needs because of the stringent focus on high-stakes testing, had little time to teach creatively, and bored themselves and their students with practice problems as they prepared for standardized testing" (Cawelti, 2006, p. 65).

"We try to give kids different ways to engage with content, but it's gotten to be so challenging," says Joann Winkler, who, like Knightly, has received awards for her creativity in teaching social studies. As a 5th grade teacher at Liberty Elementary School in Port Charlotte, Florida, Winkler finds she is constrained by demands that her instruction produce "certain kinds of data." Such outcomes require a heavy emphasis on test prep, she says. With 32 years of teaching under her belt, Winkler acknowledges that this isn't the best way to teach. Still, although she remains passionate about social studies, and although she and her colleagues would enjoy creating lessons that students find interesting and motivating, Winkler is resigned: "Our hands are tied."

It's not just teachers who find themselves bound by accountability mania, however. School leaders are also held in check. "School boards hold administrators accountable for test scores," says Jeff Passe, an education professor at the University of North Carolina at Charlotte. As a result, these administrators become "increasingly strict about when certain things should be taught."

Or *not* taught, observes Peggy Altoff, president of the National Council for the Social Studies (NCSS). She notes that subjects such as physical education, art, and music are likely to remain part of the learning program because schedules allow it: teachers are given planning time when their students are off at those classes. It's not as easy to hold social studies time sacred. In fact, says Altoff, since NCLB mandates have been in effect, "only four states report the same amount of time being spent on teaching social studies."

Some administrators who pressure teachers to spend less time teaching social studies may have been "thrust into the curriculum coordinator role" without sufficient professional development, says Roger Wolff, assistant education professor at the University of South Dakota. These administrators don't have a broad enough understanding of why it's important to incorporate social science in the curriculum.

Even administrators who do understand the importance of learning social studies may have compelling reasons for not addressing the topic. "My principal fully believes that social studies is important for students to learn—he was a high school history teacher, after all," says Elizabeth Sinclair, a 4th grade teacher at The New School in Seattle, Washington. Still, when the school was founded in 2002, its goal was to help children of color reverse a legacy of poor academic performance. As a result, the schedule and the curriculum were carefully planned to emphasize critical thinking skills and knowledge of subjects tested on the Washington Assessment of Student Learning (WASL).

Sinclair came to The New School in 2006, leaving behind a learning program that integrated social studies into a thematic curriculum. Sinclair, whose innovative social studies lessons were included in Annenberg Media's

Social Studies in Action video library, now finds it challenging enough to squeeze science into a day that emphasizes "absolute content blocks" for core subjects. "I miss [social studies] horribly," she says, but it's not on the WASL, and the pressure to help students improve performance on that test "is huge."

The Balance-Wheel: Thrown Out of Kilter

The current curricular focus in U.S. schools may result from the efforts of well-meaning policymakers and sincere educators—but we know where the road paved with good intentions leads. As Marge Scherer noted in "Perspectives: The NCLB Issue," the most positive effect of the federal law has been "the focus of attention and resources on poor and minority students, English language learners, and students with disabilities"—the so-called "invisible children"—yet "the greatest shame of a failed NCLB would be that these students will suffer more from the withholding of a rich curriculum in favor of a test-heavy education" (2006, p. 7).

It would be unfortunate if excluding social studies instruction ultimately disenfranchises the very students whom educators and policymakers are trying to advance. If school is the place where children learn what it means to be citizens in a democracy, as many experts have asserted (see "Civic Virtue in the Schools"), then students who graduate without that basic understanding could well become our future nonvoters. These students may not know that there are systems in place that give them a voice in determining how they will be governed.

Many of the students Joann Winkler teaches, for example, come from "families that aren't involved in civic activities—their parents don't vote." She believes, therefore, that it's up to her—and to public schools in general—to teach students about civic responsibility. "Social studies is such a powerful part of the curriculum—I feel it helps students practice for life," says Winkler. Through social studies, she observes, students learn "about the world they're entering, about the economic system in our country, about voting, about history and why we are what we are."

By the time students reach high school, it's already getting too late to instill these democratic and civic ideals in students, says Margit McGuire, an education professor at Seattle University. It's in elementary school that

Civic Virtue in the Schools

Like limbs that weaken from lack of use, students' democratic muscles lack vigor if they don't have a chance to use them. To halt an evident decline in civic engagement among youth, an increasing number of educators are urging U.S. schools to reinvigorate their mission to nurture democracy.

Even when civics was widespread as a school course, it generally gave students a textbook acquaintance with the three branches of government and a feeling that voting was a good thing to do. Still, young people rarely exercise the long-anticipated right to vote. U.S. Census statistics show that only 32 percent of people ages 18–24 voted in the 2000 presidential election, compared with 54.7 percent of all voting-age citizens.

"Schools need to reclaim the purpose of public education and the notion that one's education is part of a larger good and can contribute to the betterment of society," says Carl Glickman, an expert on school renewal whose new book, *Holding Sacred Ground,* examines leadership in democratic schools.

Rather than hold our schools captive with high-stakes testing, Glickman argues, we should require them to provide opportunities for students to put their learning to work in the larger community, whether that means the school or the neighborhood, the city or the state.

Also, although a student's individual goals for higher education and a career are important, schools should consider these plans as part of a larger objective to improve society and allow justice and equality to flourish, stresses Glickman.

But rejuvenating and reforming civic education won't be easy. Denee Mattioli, a past president of the National Council for the Social Studies, laments the apathy toward civic education, saying schools reflect the nation's neglect. For example, she notes, "People don't want to pay taxes for schools if their kids are grown up." Each generation needs to appreciate basic democratic values if the republic is to survive, Mattioli continues. "If people remembered and understood that charge, schools wouldn't be having to have bake sales to make sure they have enough textbooks."

Whole-School Democracy

To send a consistent message about the value of democracy, schools should not reserve its practice for students alone. Teachers, foremost, must "speak truth to power," to borrow a Quaker adage about confronting authority, says Eric Nadelstern, deputy superintendent of new and small schools for New York City's Bronx borough.

"The governance structure of the school is inextricably linked to the methods of the teachers. A 'fiat-and-memorandum' principal will have teachers dictating to kids," which squelches any democratic efforts in the classroom, Nadelstern warns. "You can't do it for kids unless you first do it for teachers."

The democratic practice encourages all teachers to question authority, even that of superintendents and the school board. "We want to empower teachers to collaborate on the curriculum, speak the truth, and question the school board," Nadelstern says. "Democracy is messy, so we're not dictating from the central office how it should be done. As long as rigorous learning connects to kids' lives, we leave it up to the local schools to decide the details."

Democracy may be a messy and complicated process, but teachers can and should teach it, practice it, and pass it on in the schools despite the effort that such a reinvigorated and nuanced civic education would require, these educators say.

"Citizenship is not just what you drop in the ballot box," says George Wood, principal at Federal Hocking High School in Stewart, Ohio. "You have to live and breathe it every single day."

Source: From "Civic Virtue in the Schools: Engaging a New Generation of Citizens," by R. Allen, 2003, *Curriculum Update,* pp. 1–8. Copyright © 2003 by Association for Supervision and Curriculum Development.

students need opportunities to practice their roles as citizens, she asserts. In these early years of schooling, teachers can start to channel a child's natural inclination to "care deeply about what is fair and just" into a deeper understanding about how to interact with others in a positive, civic way.

That won't happen if social studies is "relegated to a third or fourth spot," contends Roger Wolff. Instead, he says, schools will be graduating a "whole decade of students who are not versed in and instilled with dispositions for civic action."

There is concern, too, for older students' academic performance. According to Jeff Passe, "High school teachers are just beginning to see kids—especially children from low-income areas—who have had nominal social studies. Instruction has been minimal and shallow." As a result, these students must work harder to meet tougher demands. It's the nature of schooling to "move from the simple to the more complex, to build from the familiar to the unfamiliar," says Mark Stout, the social studies curriculum coordinator for Maryland's Howard County Public School System. "If kids are missing big chunks [of social studies content], they aren't going to be ready for the rigor that's expected in high school."

This situation has been characterized as "an unintended consequence of NCLB," says Peggy Altoff. If that's true, she maintains, "then someone has to do something intentional about it—now!"

First Amendment Schools

Seventeen First Amendment project schools throughout the United States are exploring ways for students to better understand their roles as citizens in a democracy as they learn a deeper practical appreciation of the five freedoms of the First Amendment (religion, speech, press, assembly, and petition). Projects at these schools, funded through the collaboration of the Freedom Forum's First Amendment Center and ASCD, will serve as models that other schools can adapt to their own communities. For more information about the First Amendment Schools project, visit www.firstamendmentschools.org.

Is Integration the Answer?

It's too late to restore social studies to a prominent place in the curriculum, asserts Alan Haskvitz, a veteran middle school teacher who pens a regular column for EdNews.org. "That war was over the moment NCLB was passed," he writes in "The Disrespecting of Social Studies" (2006). What's needed now, Haskvitz states, is for teachers to address social studies subject matter while teaching other subjects, such as math and language arts. Teachers must also "avoid the pre-fabricated lesson plan in favor of teachable moments and integrated lessons," he maintains.

Although many educators agree with Haskvitz's assertion, effectively integrating the curriculum and incorporating timely issues into lessons is a learned art, and teachers often have few opportunities to develop that ability. According to Roger Wolff, it's a stumbling block that teacher education programs could begin to address.

At the University of South Dakota, for example, Wolff and two colleagues worked together to align social studies standards with those of other content areas. Together, the three education professors—representing social studies, math, and science—taught an integrated unit, and then asked their students to create such a unit of their own. "We asked students to look at the disciplines and find the connections, to see how [the subjects] are all related," Wolff explains. As students go through the process, there is a definite "aha" moment as they discover how rich learning can be when activities intertwine different content areas.

As a result of his integrated unit, Wolff is confident that the students who graduate from his program will know how to infuse social studies into their teaching. Graduates of the program, he says, "have gone out into school systems and have been asked by their administrators to assist faculties in aligning standards and apply that process to curriculum design—in their first year of teaching. We therefore feel very good that the process has helped them."

"Whenever you get a team of teachers working on the express goal of integrating the curriculum in a meaningful way, the result is an excellent product," says Jeff Passe. Unfortunately, he acknowledges, many states and districts have adopted scripted textbooks and instructional approaches that don't allow for teacher collaboration on curriculum and lesson planning.

Yet social studies can be used to bolster skills in other subject areas, such as English. Passe advises showing teachers "how the subject is a vocabulary engine" and how nonfiction texts—such as newspaper and magazine articles, information on Web sites, and textbooks—can help students learn to analyze what they read.

Teachers in Prince George's County Public Schools in Maryland have found that reading and social studies instruction pair nicely together. Teachers know to emphasize reading skills when teaching the content, says Kara Libby, supervisor of social studies for the district. Students need practice reading informational texts because it is a testable skill, she points out. Indeed, about 70 percent of the questions on the Maryland School Assessment require students to comprehend informational texts, and many of those questions focus on social studies. "We say to social studies teachers, 'When you teach the content, use pre- and post-reading strategies,'" Libby explains. "'Look at the vocabulary and discuss it.'"

Betsy Bratek and her colleagues at Greenbelt Middle School in Prince George's County "do a lot with anticipation guides," she says. Before her 6th graders read a specific passage, Bratek gives them a list of statements. The students then have to determine whether the facts she presents are correct. "I ask students to think about what information they will need to support their answers," she explains. "They know they have to find examples in the text."

"Breaking down the text is key," agrees Christina Doepel, social studies department chair at G. James Gholson Middle School in Prince George's County. "Asking children to read six or seven pages is too overwhelming for them." She adds that it's also important to use activities that allow students "to get their hands involved."

To review social studies vocabulary, for example, Doepel's students create *foldables*—small books that result from folding paper in a particular way. In addition to writing definitions, students draw pictures that help them remember the concepts associated with the vocabulary words. "I've used this activity with students K–8, and they all love it," Doepel says. "Even older kids still like art."

In addition to facilitating reading instruction, social studies can be used to provide new insights into mathematical concepts. Although "the complaint from math students through the ages has been that math is not relevant," notes Passe, there is actually such "rich mathematical data in every social studies book that students can't help but see the relevance of math." In geography, for example, when students compare and contrast early Spanish and Iroquois housing, they consider how the environment was used to construct the houses, says Gale Ekiss, co-coordinator of the Arizona Geographic Alliance. To extend the lesson, younger students could log the number of triangles and squares that abound in each structure, while older students explore how builders used perimeter and area to construct each type of house.

This lesson, based on national and state standards, is typical of the 85 that are included in GeoMath, a resource "developed by teachers for teachers" with the Arizona Geographic Alliance in response to the frustration teachers felt at not having enough time to teach social studies. "Teachers want to teach geography," Ekiss asserts; they just need a means for doing so. GeoMath, she says, has everything a teacher needs to address social studies and math, including an outline of how each lesson aligns with standards for each subject area. That way, should an administrator ask, the teacher can show how delivering a lesson on earthquakes gives students a chance to hone math skills; for example, students might be analyzing data on seismicity to determine whether their state is more or less susceptible to earthquakes.

The Arizona Geographic Alliance also worked with teachers to create GeoLiteracy, a program that integrates geography standards with those for reading and writing. The lessons feature geography content, while the reading and writing standards guide the assessments. One lesson, for example, introduces 4th and 5th grade students to the ancient city of Jerusalem and asks them to consider why the city has an important place in the modern world. To assess learning for that lesson, students answer questions that were written to mirror the style of those found on Arizona's state tests.

Data on the effectiveness of the program, which was piloted in 20 Arizona school districts, reveal that the lessons "made a difference in reading comprehension," Ekiss states. Of the 5,000 students who participated, 85 percent scored 80 percent or higher on the state geography assessment, 84 percent scored 80 percent or higher on the reading assessment, and 78 percent scored 80 percent or higher on the writing assessment (Arizona Geographic Alliance, 2002).

Such results don't happen by chance, says Ekiss. The lessons are successful because everything a teacher needs is included: "The lesson is there, the map is there, the graph is there," Ekiss observes. "The assessment is there, along with instructions on how to grade it." She maintains that such standardized lesson plans enable a teacher to look at a lesson one day and teach it the next.

Curricular materials like GeoMath and GeoLiteracy can help teachers challenge the "power of NCLB to push social studies out of the curriculum," agrees Margit McGuire. Yet there are caveats to consider. The good news is that many publishers now use social studies content to reinforce math and literacy, she says; the bad news is that some of those programs are "taught totally as a literacy program."

During national presentations she gives on this trend, McGuire shares samples of materials that have a social studies theme—such as making a new nation—but whose activities are designed to hone literacy skills. The social studies in the materials is addressed "in a pretty superficial way," she says, adding that busy teachers with precious little time may use the materials and then think that they've taught social studies. "It's simply not enough to have students read about making a nation," McGuire asserts. Teachers need to extend students' thinking, to guide their students into considering what the story suggests their role in a democracy might be. "While there is more fabulous literature than ever before, it's not enough to treat a literacy experience as social studies unless you come back to the underlying message and look at it in terms of what can we learn to make us a better citizen," McGuire contends.

Getting Political

If social studies is preparation for citizenship, as educators like McGuire assert, then "that's the argument we have to make to policymakers," says Jeff Passe, who finds that the majority of policymakers "are shocked" to learn about the marginalization of social studies. "It just never occurred to them that this would take place," he observes.

Passe and others active in the social studies arena now actively advocate for their subject. "People talk politics like never before in social studies circles," observes Passe, who is lobbying hard to ensure that each state has a supervisor of social studies. Policymakers need to hear why the subject is important and why teachers need training, he notes, and "the absence of social studies supervisors prevents the quality teaching that we can achieve."

Such a position at the district level can also be an antidote to atrophy. "I feel that there has been a resurgence for social studies in the last couple of years," says Christina Doepel, who welcomes the presence of a social studies supervisor in the district office. "We're fortunate that somebody in our county is looking out for social studies. I think you need supervisors to make sure social studies is not forgotten. Our county sees the value that social studies has in helping children become well developed and well rounded."

Reflections   ◆ ◆ ◆

Social studies educators are now activists for their subject. Now, more than ever, advocacy is a responsibility that all educators must shoulder. Educators must continue to remind policymakers and the public about the purposes of education in a democratic society. Peggy Altoff notes that "there is a lack of understanding of what social studies really is" (see "Viewpoint: An Interview with Denee Mattioli"). "Some individuals in content areas have spent a lifetime bashing social studies. We now have an opportunity for all separate content organizations to recognize our commonalities rather than emphasize our differences. We can worry about the differences once we know the content is being taught."

At which point Horace Mann can rest easy.

Viewpoint:
An Interview with Denee Mattioli

Why do you think people have a hard time defining social studies?

When I was in the classroom, everything from bicycle safety to fire prevention week was put under social studies. Many of those are very valuable programs, but instead of looking at them and saying this should be in an after-school program or with some other organization, special interest groups have slipped them under the heading of social studies—especially in districts that lack a well-defined curriculum. This further confuses what social studies is about.

At the National Council for the Social Studies (NCSS), we look at the curriculum areas—history, geography, economics, political science, and so on—and ask, "Why do students need to study these areas?" We're looking for a curriculum that will prepare students for the role of participating and contributing citizens in a democratic republic. To know our heritage and geography, to be economically responsible and savvy, and to make wise decisions based on information— all of that has to do with being a good citizen. That's all social studies. Many policymakers and the general public have lost sight of the original purpose of public education in the United States, which is to prepare citizens. That's why our Founding Fathers came up with this terrific idea of free, universal education.

How do you answer those at the Fordham Foundation who say that social studies has become increasingly ideological and vague and that we need to go back to the basics by giving students a firm base in U.S. history?

I think we can use the analogy that if we as a nation of educators are parents and all the curricular areas are our children—if two of them are hungry, we feed them. We don't starve the other children to make sure these two are fed. Certainly, rigorous, academic content standards are necessary—but not just history or not just American history. We feel that to reach the goal of being a strong contributing citizen, you need knowledge in many areas. Definitely we need citizens who are knowledgeable about our own heritage, but also are able to set that heritage in the context of the world. They also need to have economic knowledge, civics, and political knowledge in order to be good citizens and make sure that this gem of history, the United States, not just survives but thrives.

Papers from Fordham like "Where Did Social Studies Go Wrong?" are not organized research but a series of individually written opinion essays. They come from one particular perspective. Some of the authors came up with very good points—yes, we do need to improve knowledge and understanding in the social sciences. The test scores, however, aren't the goal. Test scores report on whether we are reaching our goal. To continue to just criticize what's going on without really working to help make a change come about is problematic.

What can we do for social studies teachers struggling with the possible marginalization of their curriculum due to No Child Left Behind (NCLB)?

We need to listen to the teachers who are finding ways of dealing with the pressures of NCLB. We have some absolutely incredible things going on in education across this nation and at every level. We have knowledgeable, dedicated teachers whose students are doing a phenomenal job of not only learning and doing well on tests, but impacting students' knowledge outside the classroom. What we need to do is find out exactly what works through research and then learn from that research so that other teachers can use it. We also need to know why certain methodologies don't work with particular populations of students. We need to know more about how children learn—what motivates them—and that should inform how we instruct.

Denee Mattioli is a past president of the National Council for the Social Studies.

Source: From "Viewpoint: An Interview with Denee Mattioli," by L. Varlas, 2004, *Curriculum Technology Quarterly.* Copyright © 2004 by Association for Supervision and Curriculum Development.

Exploring Standards and Themes in Social Studies

2

There is a reality in the social studies field that "nobody has wanted to talk about," observes Margit McGuire: there is just too much to teach. Consider all the subjects that social studies encompasses: geography, history, economics, civics, anthropology, sociology. "When you stack them all up, you get a pretty thick set of standards," McGuire notes. "It's not humanly possible to teach all those standards—not unless we have the students for a lifetime."

In response to this dilemma, some educators have started to look anew at the depth and breadth of social studies learning goals. A task force formed by the National Council for the Social Studies (NCSS) has been charged with determining whether social studies standards need revision and, accordingly, has conducted surveys, reviewed appropriate literature, and held hearings at the 2006 NCSS annual conference. The working group will ultimately present its recommendations to the NCSS board of directors.

Published in 1994, the current standards are designed to guide teachers, school systems, and states in developing their own social studies curricula, Jeff Passe explains. Rather than offering a "laundry list of objectives," he says, the standards identify universal themes and performance expectations at different grade levels. Educators can then create lessons in a particular subject area—whether it's history, civics, or geography—that illuminate a theme while addressing content standards (see "Curriculum Standards for Social Studies," p. 16).

Emphasizing enduring understandings rather than specific content encourages integration, says Peggy Altoff. "It's hard to teach anything that's just history," she notes. When studying a historical event, students

Curriculum Standards for Social Studies

An Orchestral Arrangement

To best understand how to use the NCSS standards for social studies, think of how an orchestra makes beautiful music, the standards' authors advise. An orchestra consists of an ensemble of different instruments, with musical arrangements that are unique to those instruments. For a given musical composition, for example, the French horn may lead while the violins, cellos, trumpets, and wood-winds play supporting roles. For a different composition, a different instrument may lead.

Social studies is also an ensemble, one made up of various disciplines. One learning goal may require that a lesson focus on a specific discipline, such as history; another learning goal may integrate several disciplines, showing students how history, geography, and economics are interrelated, for example. Just as a music composer determines how instruments work individually or together within a piece of music, curriculum designers, including teachers, determine whether a lesson will emphasize a single discipline or several. The composer asks the audience to explore a musical landscape that he or she has created; the curriculum designer asks students to explore a particular theme (see "Ten Thematic Strands in Social Studies").

Just as a musical composition is a whole, with the individual instruments helping to convey an artistic message, the social studies standards address "overall curriculum design and comprehensive student performance expectations, while the individual discipline standards (civics and government, economics, geography, and history) provide focused and enhanced content detail" (The Task Force of the National Council for the Social Studies, 1994, p. viii).

Source: From *Expectations of Excellence: Curriculum Standards for Social Studies,* by the Task Force of the National Council for the Social Studies, 1994. Copyright © 1994 by National Council for the Social Studies. Adapted with permission.

Ten Thematic Strands in Social Studies

Ten themes make up the NCSS standards' framework, drawing on one or more relevant disciplines. The theme of *culture,* for example, can include the disciplines of anthropology, geography, history, and sociology. Curriculum designers are responsible for determining how to help students explore the theme from one or more of those disciplines. When creating curriculum and lesson plans, most educators look to the content standards for the various disciplines and align them with the social studies' learning goals.

The 10 themes include

- Culture
- Time, Continuity, and Change
- People, Places, and Environments
- Individual Development and Identity
- Individuals, Groups, and Institutions
- Power, Authority, and Governance
- Production, Distribution, and Consumption
- Science, Technology, and Society
- Global Connections
- Civic Ideals and Practices

look at more than the *who* and the *when* and the *where;* for example, students often study the economic implications of an event. "When you look at the people, events, and stories that you examine as content, you can't help but go across [subject-area] standards," says Altoff.

That approach still holds up, according to Passe. He believes that task force members will recommend that the standards' technology performance expectations be updated and that other themes be tweaked a little, but that the existing set of principles be maintained. He also hopes that the task force members recommend that the social studies standards acknowledge how the curriculum has narrowed as a result of No Child Left Behind. Many state-level educators are reluctant to admit the extent to which social studies learning has been hindered by prioritizing other disciplines, like math and science, says Passe. Although some states may present "a really wonderful document" of social studies expectations, only a small number of those objectives can be met. It's time for more honesty, Passe asserts: "We're fooling the public [by assuring them] that kids are getting this great social studies education."

Striving for Inclusion and Balance

If educators create social studies learning expectations that are "a little more realistic," as Passe suggests, then the challenge becomes, Whose reality do we draw on?

"When the standards were originally written, the authors asked, 'What is central to social studies? What is it we want people to know and understand?' " adds Margit McGuire. "The question that wasn't asked was, 'What can we leave out?' "

That's a tough question to answer. So many different groups vie for a spot in the curriculum—the Veterans of Foreign Wars, survivors of the Holocaust and their families, minority groups active in the quest for civil rights. "The list goes on and on," says McGuire. There are so many stories to tell, and "you can't say to these groups, 'Your story isn't worthy to be in the standards.' "

What you *can* say to these groups is that inclusion is always the goal, however difficult it may be to achieve. For such exchanges, actions often speak louder than words. "We really try to respond to groups who feel their story isn't told," says Mark Stout of Howard County Public Schools. Stout meets regularly with community members to listen. "The African American community, the Muslim community, and so on—each of these groups has a legitimate cause for what should be taught," Stout says. His job is to reassure: "We are trying to be inclusive and balance their stories with the traditional canon." Yet he also points out that schools must follow the state standards and focus on helping students gain the skills they need to pass the Maryland High School Assessment in government—a necessary step for graduation.

In states like Maryland, a culminating assessment helps identify for districts and schools what social studies content is important to learn. But even in states that don't have a social studies assessment, the students' ideal end state should be kept foremost in mind. "Curriculum and assessment gurus don't ask, 'What do we leave out?' We talk, instead, about the focus. 'What are the power standards? What do you want every kid to know and do?' " says Altoff, who is also the district supervisor for social studies in Colorado Springs, Colorado.

It's the districts that decide what stories will be included to address the standards, she explains, and those decisions are influenced by the demographics of the community. Because there is a significant Hispanic population in Colorado Springs, for example, it's important that students from these families "see their stories in our curriculum," Altoff states. In another community, the selection of course titles and materials may reflect a different population. In Philadelphia, for example, students must take a course in African American history to qualify for graduation.

Achieving balance among the disciplines and competing stories will always be a work in progress, adds McGuire—and change is slow. "Social studies, honestly, is quite conservative," she observes, explaining that the "love of subject" makes it difficult for educators to objectively decide what content "we ultimately let go."

Curriculum historian Ronald Evans would agree with McGuire. "In the social studies wars, the traditional discipline-based approaches seem to have staying power," he writes (2006, p. 321). He points to well-financed advocacy groups as powerful guarantors of adherence to a traditional K–12 social studies canon.

Still, Evans reminds teachers that they have choices. They can choose what to emphasize in their classrooms so long as they "examine the alternatives and develop their rationales and teaching practices thoroughly." A well-reasoned argument for what they want to include will help teachers "defend the integrity of the field" and retain the freedom they need to make well-informed curricular decisions, Evans asserts. After all, this autonomy is "the essence of professional practice in education" (2006, p. 320).

Informed Choices, Meaningful Lessons

Helping educators make reasoned choices has been Mary McFarland's job for some years now. Pick a theme, any theme, and she can show you how to align a lesson with that topic while at the same time emphasizing one or more disciplines and addressing specific content and processes. Featured in Annenberg Media's *Social Studies in Action* video series, McFarland is an education consultant who once served as social studies director for the Parkway School District in St. Louis, Missouri. In the video, McFarland works with Boston-area elementary teachers as they strive to answer what she describes as the toughest question they'll face as social studies educators: With so many possibilities, what do we teach?

Keeping this question in mind, the workshop participants watch scenes from a kindergarten class in which students explore production, distribution, and consumption—one of the 10 social studies themes laid out by the NCSS standards. The class begins with a review of a book called *Pasta Please* by Melvin Berger and Lisa Trumbauer (1994). The book describes the different roles that workers have when making pasta in a factory, as well as the importance of working together on the assembly line. "What is it called when we work together?" the teacher asks. "Cooperation," several students reply. The students then form their own assembly line in the classroom to make bread.

As the students experience firsthand the need for cooperation to create a product efficiently, they also consider how technology can affect the process. While the children work together on their bread, ingredients are being added to a bread machine in the corner of the classroom. "Which one will be done first?" the teacher asks. Most students answer, correctly, that the bread in the machine will be done first. This lesson lays the initial foundation for understanding the influence of science and technology on the workplace.

This lesson, McFarland points out in the video, shows how teachers can use one discipline (economics) to help students explore a concept (cooperation) through a social studies theme (production, distribution, and consumption). If the teacher had wanted to, she could have easily integrated other subjects into the lesson, including math and reading. But in this case, the teacher chose a single discipline focus (see Figure 2.1).

McFarland's workshop participants then watch a video of another classroom lesson. In this example, K–1 students examine the many ways in which people observe the winter holidays. The teacher reads a book about the winter solstice, which helps the students see that light is a common feature of many winter celebrations. "Why do so many communities celebrate light at the same time?" the teacher asks. "Because December is a dark month, and darkness is scary," several students reply.

FIGURE 2.1
Social Studies in Action: A Methodology Workshop, K–5

4: Applying Themes and Disciplines—Viewing Chart
As you watch, list the NCSS themes and related disciplines each teacher is building on in her lesson. Then list the concepts and processes being taught.

	Lesson	Theme	Discipline	Concepts/Processes
Teacher #1	**Making Bread Together:** This kindergarten class creates an assembly line and studies needs and wants.	• Production, Distribution, and Consumption	• Economics	Cooperation/ Cooperative learning
Teacher #2	**Celebrations of Light:** This K–1 class studies the common thread in holiday celebrations among different cultures.	• Culture • Time, Continuity, and Change • People, Places, and Environments	• Anthropology • History • Geography	We are different, but alike/Literature and multiple intelligences–based work stations

Source: From Social Studies in Action: A Methodology Workshop, K–5, 2003. Copyright © 2003 by WGBH Educational Foundation. Adapted with permission. Retrieved December 28, 2006, from www.learner.org/channel/workshops/socialstudies/pdf/session4/viewing_chart.pdf

"The people need hope," says another student. After the class discussion, the children move to several multiple intelligences–based centers (word-smart, math-smart, self-smart, picture-smart, and so on) that provide an array of activities enabling students to further explore the concepts through their different learning strengths.

This lesson addresses several themes and disciplines, McFarland notes in the video. The students study geography as they consider why some parts of the world are darker in December than in any other month of the year. They become anthropologists as they learn about the traditions and beliefs of particular groups of people. History is incorporated as the students consider the origins of winter celebrations and discuss how these events have evolved through the years. The lesson touches on at least three social studies themes, including culture; time, continuity, and change; and people, places, and environments (see Figure 2.2).

According to McFarland, the lessons she features in her workshop illustrate how the readily adaptable NCSS themes can help teachers create content-rich, discipline-based lessons. When teachers create such learning experiences, they "bring their own intelligence to the standards," says McFarland. In using the NCSS standards, she notes, teachers should consider "their own contexts" when answering the question, What should we teach? That was the main intention when the standards were originally written, says McFarland, and it's an approach that she hopes will be "retained forever."

Toward Deeper Understanding

In identifying 10 broad, interrelated themes and suggesting how students might express their understanding of those themes, the NCSS standards task force recommends an approach to curriculum development and instructional planning that pairs well with Understanding by Design (UbD). UbD "encourages teachers to develop motivating, engaging activities that help students explore, reflect on, and revisit big ideas, key concepts, and essential questions over time" (Seif, 2003/2004, p. 58). As with the NCSS standards, UbD asks teachers to first identify what they want students to know and be able to do. Then teachers create lessons and

FIGURE 2.2

Social Studies in Action: A Methodology Workshop, K–5

4: Applying Themes and Disciplines—Graphic Organizer
Review the NCSS themes and related academic disciplines, then list concepts and processes you teach.
Note: A concept is a topic and a process is a way of examining a topic.

NCSS Themes	Related Disciplines	Concepts and Processes
Culture *Traditions, beliefs, and values*	Anthropology	Example: Colonial America/ artifacts
Time, Continuity, and Change *Stability and change over time*	History	
People, Places, and Environments *Spatial concepts and relationships*	Geography, Anthropology	
Individual Development and Identity *Personal identity, cultural contexts*	Psychology	
Individuals, Groups, and Institutions *Relationships among groups, institutions, and individuals*	Sociology	
Power, Authority, and Governance *Structure and variety of governments*	Political Science	
Production, Distribution, and Consumption *Decisions about resources*	Economics	
Science, Technology, and Society *Influence of science and technology*	History, Sociology, Science	
Global Connections *Links between peoples and societies*	History, Economics, Geography, Anthropology	
Civic Ideals and Practices *Values, ideals, and practices*	Political Science, History, Sociology	

After you have completed the graphic organizer, review your answers and consider the following questions:

1. How was this similar to or different from the way you organize your curriculum?
2. How can NCSS themes and disciplines guide your teaching?

Source: From *Social Studies in Action: A Methodology Workshop, K–5,* 2003. Copyright © 2003 by WGBH Educational Foundation. Reprinted with permission. Retrieved December 28, 2006, from www.learner.org/channel/workshops/socialstudies/pdf/session4/graphic_organizer.pdf

> # Give It a Try!
>
> *Make a copy of "4: Applying Themes and Disciplines—Graphic Orga-*
> *nizer." Now read the following lesson description and determine the*
> *themes and disciplines that are addressed. What are the concepts and*
> *processes used?*
>
> A 5th grade class is studying American Indian tribes. After a
> whole-class review of previous activities, which included a discussion
> of reasons why tribes might have migrated (weather, food supply,
> and so on), the class splits into groups of four to read the next sec-
> tion from their textbook.
>
> The teacher reminds students of the four roles to be delegated
> to the members of each group:
>
> - **Organizer:** Works with group members to ensure that each
> has a job.
> - **Recorder:** Writes down the information that the group must
> present to the class.
> - **Reader:** Reads the text passage aloud to the rest of the
> group. (Note: As the reader reads about an American Indian tribe,
> the group members must identify the area in which the tribe lived
> and the kinds of things that tribe members needed while they lived
> in that area. Ultimately, the group will locate the area on a map and
> then cut out the items that "fit" with the group's tribe from three
> pages of artifacts.)
> - **Presenter:** Presents information discovered by the group to
> the class.

assessments designed specifically to help students reach that end point
(see "Understanding by Design at a Glance," p. 25).

This backward design model has been used successfully by several
schools in Bucks County, Pennsylvania, to update their social studies
programs. In the Quakertown Community School District, for example, the curriculum revision task force decided to use a framework

Understanding by Design at a Glance

Understanding by Design (UbD) is the brainchild of Grant Wiggins and Jay McTighe, experts in the field of curriculum, assessment, and teaching for understanding. Through the UbD framework, Wiggins and McTighe have attempted to synthesize the best practices and the research-driven design principles associated with teaching and assessing for understanding. The UbD framework emphasizes a backward design process and involves three interrelated stages:

- **Stage One:** Identify desired results (such as enduring understandings, essential questions, and enabling knowledge objectives).
- **Stage Two:** Determine acceptable evidence to assess and to evaluate student achievement of desired results.
- **Stage Three:** Design learning activities to promote all students' mastery of desired results and their subsequent success on identified assessment tasks.

UbD is not a program to be implemented, Wiggins and McTighe assert. Rather, the framework helps educators create learning experiences that foster deep understanding. Students demonstrate their knowledge through one or more of the following six facets of understanding:

- **Explanation:** The ability to demonstrate, derive, describe, design, justify, or prove something using evidence.
- **Interpretation:** The ability to create something new from learned knowledge—for example, to formulate a critique, create analogies and metaphors, draw inferences, construct meaning, translate, make predictions, or form hypotheses.
- **Application:** The ability to use learned knowledge in new, unique, or unpredictable situations and contexts—for example, to build, create, invent, perform, produce, solve, or test.
- **Perspective:** The ability to analyze and draw conclusions about contrasting viewpoints on a given event, topic, or situation.

- **Empathy:** The capacity to walk in another's shoes—for example, to participate in role-play, describe another's emotions, or analyze and justify someone else's reactions.
- **Self-Knowledge:** The ability to self-examine, self-reflect, self-evaluate, express reflective insight, and monitor and modify one's own comprehension of information and events.

Educators who have worked extensively with the UbD framework almost universally acknowledge its commonsense recommendations for (1) unpacking curriculum standards; (2) emphasizing students' understanding, not just formulaic recall; (3) expanding assessment tools and repertoires to create a photo album of student achievement instead of a snapshot; and (4) incorporating the best of what current research tells us about meeting the needs of all learners.

Source: From *Making the Most of Understanding by Design,* by J. Brown, 2004. Copyright © 2004 by Association for Supervision and Curriculum Development.

of enduring understandings and essential questions to guide the K–12 social studies plan:

> The group [revising the program] began with the district's K–12 social studies standards, a document closely paralleling the standards developed by the National Council for the Social Studies (1994). After considerable brainstorming, discussion, and debate, the group developed a set of enduring understandings and essential questions for each standards theme. For example, for the cultural theme, teachers decided on the following enduring understanding: "Cultural similarities and differences exist because of physical and social environments. Recognizing these similarities and differences promotes understanding." This understanding gave rise to a number of essential questions: Can societies erase racial division? Does cultural diversity enhance the quality of one's life? How does the environment affect culture? (Seif, 2003/2004, pp. 55, 57)

Using the K–12 framework, teachers created course- and unit-based understandings and questions. For example, an 8th grade U.S. History unit titled Early Modern Europe: Exploration and Enlightenment now focuses on such essential questions as, What happens when cultures meet?, How does one culture evaluate the morality of another culture?, What kinds of interactions benefit humanity?, and What kinds of interactions create conflict?

A later 8th grade unit, Regional Development of the United States, 1800–1850, has a different set of essential questions: What effects do a nation's resources have on its development? How have societies adapted to meet changing needs? How do people get what they need and what they want?

Such questions encourage students to explore big ideas, which is one of the major benefits of the Understanding by Design model. When students learn about the signing of the Magna Carta, for example, they will not see it as "some discrete event that they will soon forget"; rather, they will explore the topic as it relates to larger ideas, such as the rule of law and due process, observes Seif. In addition, "to determine whether students can apply the knowledge and skills they have learned within authentic and relevant contexts," assessments go well beyond multiple-choice and fill-in-the-blank questions. Teachers might ask students to create a museum that focuses on the development of the rule of law, for example. Students would have to explain why they would include the Magna Carta in the museum and write a narrative about the Magna Carta as part of the museum display (Seif, 2003/2004, pp. 54–55).

So Much to Teach, So Little Time

Given all that social studies encompasses, and given the trend toward a narrowing curriculum, many educators have thought long and hard about how to ensure that students still gain a solid, basic understanding of social studies concepts.

Some advocate aligning themes with standards for specific disciplines; others start with identifying enduring understandings and planning with the end in mind. For any of these approaches to be effective, educators can't merely ask, What can we teach? They also need to ask,

What kinds of learning and assessment activities will promote students' deep understanding of social studies content? and How can we create experiences that lend coherence to social studies learning, K–12?

The NCSS standards can be used as a guide for educators wrestling with those questions, asserts Mary McFarland. "Curriculum development goes through phases," she observes. A high degree of integration predominates through the elementary grades, but as students progress through the grade levels, the disciplines become more distinct, she explains. The standards can inform both approaches as students progress through school: "There are themes, they are linked to other themes, and they can be integrated. At the same time, each of the themes ties closely to the academic disciplines."

The standards also provide "a sense of the field . . . a sense of the fullness, K–12," says McFarland. "Social studies [learning] starts early and it starts fully—it isn't just ancillary to everything else." She acknowledges that national and state tests and curriculum crowding complicate the situation. Still, she believes that educators have an obligation to go through the process of thinking about the learning program, reviewing the standards, and then "deciding what they think their students need to learn in relation to these standards."

Reflections   ◆ ◆ ◆

"Most states have far too many content standards," asserts assessment guru W. James Popham (2006, p. 88). Popham suggests that states revise content standards "so they represent curricular aims that teachers can truly teach in the instructional time available and that they can assess in a way that pays off instructionally" (p. 88). Certainly, educators like Peggy Altoff agree with Popham's conclusion. In her district, teachers have begun to identify a smaller number of power standards. For those educators in states that have "too-numerous curricular aims," however, it's time for a little activism, writes Popham: "You need to apply whatever pressure you can, personally or in collaboration with colleagues, so that state educators immediately review these aims and, if necessary, revise them" (p. 88).

Bringing the Curriculum to Life Through Instruction and Assessment

3

A teacher who is attempting to teach without inspiring the pupil with a desire to learn is hammering on cold iron.

—*Horace Mann*

Social studies is one fascinating subject. It's the story of conflict and conquest, the study of communities and the people who live in them, the analysis of both local and global issues. With all this wonderfully dramatic material, social studies lessons can be spellbinding.

Just ask Joann Winkler's students at Liberty Elementary School in Port Charlotte, Florida. To learn more about Florida's history, Winkler's 4th and 5th grade students partnered with park rangers to research famous state sites. In addition to conducting independent research, students sent disposable cameras to the rangers and asked them to take pictures of their sites. The photos, along with various brochures and pamphlets, became part of a Tour of Florida display designed by the class. Students also created three-dimensional models of the sites and a large mural map of Florida to be displayed in the hallway. They became experts on their historic locations so that when other classes and family members took the Tour of Florida, the students were more than ready to serve as guides.

This project infused schoolwork with a sense of purpose, something Winkler wished she'd had more of when she was a student. "I didn't like school very much—it was boring, and I didn't see a connection to the real world," she says. Rather than complain, Winkler decided to do something about it. For more than 32 years now, she has dedicated herself to helping reluctant students find success in school. Indeed, Winkler notes that a pleasant side benefit of the Tour of Florida project was changing colleagues' opinions of her students' capabilities. "One teacher could not believe how much knowledge my low-performing students displayed," she recalls.

Winkler's innovative teaching brought her recognition from the National Council for the Social Studies (NCSS), which in 2004 named her the top elementary social studies teacher in the United States. The learning experiences she designs reflect the vision for effective teaching described in the NCSS standards (see "A Vision of Powerful Social Studies Teaching and Learning"). The Tour of Florida project, for example, was meaningful and active and included an authentic culminating assignment that encouraged students to think deeply and apply their learning. As a result, observes Winkler, students developed crucial skills that they will use for the rest of their lives.

A Vision of Powerful Social Studies Teaching and Learning

Social studies teaching and learning are powerful when they are meaningful, integrative, value-based, challenging, and active.

Meaningful
Meaningful learning activities emphasize authentic activities and assessment tasks. For example, instead of labeling a map, students could plan a travel route and sketch landscapes that a traveler might see on the route. Instead of listing the amendments in the Bill of Rights, students could discuss the implications of the Bill of Rights for a defendant in a given court case. Instead of writing down the definition of a principle being studied, students could use the principle to make predictions about a related situation or to guide their strategies in a simulation game.

Integrative

Social studies crosses disciplinary boundaries. Its content is anchored by themes, generalizations, and concepts drawn from the foundational disciplines, supplemented by ideas drawn from the arts, sciences, and humanities; from current events and local examples; and from students' own experiences. Social studies provides opportunities for students to read and study text materials, appreciate art and literature, communicate orally and in writing, make observations and take measurements, develop and display data, and conduct inquiry and synthesize findings using knowledge and skills taught in multiple school subjects.

Value-Based

Social studies builds in students a concern for the common good. Effective social studies teachers ensure that students become aware of the values, complexities, and dilemmas surrounding a given issue; consider the costs and benefits to the various groups involved in potential courses of action; and develop well-reasoned positions consistent with basic democratic social and political values. Students become more articulate about their own and others' policy recommendations and supporting rationales.

Challenging

To stimulate and challenge students' thinking, effective teachers expose them to multiple information sources that provide varying perspectives on topics and conflicting opinions on controversial issues. Teachers pose questions that call for thoughtful examination of the content and allow sufficient time for students to think and formulate responses and to elaborate on their peers' responses. Teachers show interest in and respect for students' thinking but demand well-reasoned arguments rather than opinions voiced without adequate thought or commitment. Teachers may sometimes challenge students' assumptions or help students identify misconceptions, flaws in their arguments, or unrecognized complications. At all times, teachers make it clear that the purpose of such a challenge is not to put students on the spot but to help them construct new understanding through thoughtful dialogue.

Active

Learning is active when the curriculum emphasizes hands-on and minds-on activities that require students to react to what they are learning and use it for some authentic purpose. In an active learning setting, students frequently engage in cooperative learning, construct three-dimensional models, dramatically re-create historical events that shaped democratic values or civic policies, and participate in role-play and simulation activities (e.g., mock trials, family interviews, data collection in the local community, and so on). Students also take on various social and civic roles, such as discussing home safety or energy conservation checklists with parents and planning appropriate follow-up action, participating in student government activities and local community restoration or improvement efforts, and volunteering at nursing homes or for political campaigns.

Source: From *Expectations of Excellence: Curriculum Standards for Social Studies,* by the Task Force of the National Council for the Social Studies, 1994. Copyright © 1994 by National Council for the Social Studies. Adapted with permission.

So Long, Joe Friday

Educators like Winkler want to instill in their students a passion for social studies, and they do so by creating learning activities that excite rather than bore. Don't give students a worksheet and ask them to scour a textbook for the word or phrase that fills in the blank, says Kathleen Waffle, principal at John F. Kennedy Elementary School in Newark, California. Instead, ask students to come up with a research question and let them "sift through the information" they uncover. Rather than asking students to memorize years and facts, "teach them research skills—that's much more important," Waffle asserts.

Better still, help students see how a social studies education can prepare them for a real-world job—that of a historian or an anthropologist, for example. When she taught 5th grade at John Muir Elementary School in San Bruno, California, Waffle wanted her students to experience the work of a museum curator whose job it was to choose items for an exhibit. She lined a table with blue fabric and gave groups of students five or six items to identify and interpret. "The students had to figure out what era the items were from, what they were made of, how they were made, and so on," Waffle explains. "Some students would sketch what they saw; other students used a matrix to help them organize their thoughts. I wanted students to get the hands-on experience of trying to figure out what artifacts can tell us" about the people who used the items and about the times in which they lived. When students shared their theories about the items they analyzed, some were "really close" to correctly identifying certain items and their uses, Waffle says.

In another hands-on activity, videotaped for Annenberg Media's *Social Studies in Action* series, Waffle asked students to analyze primary-source documents to identify business strategies used by a successful silversmith who lived in Colonial Williamsburg, Virginia. Working in groups, students reviewed a contract between the silversmith and an apprentice and then wrote an advertisement for the apprentice position based on the contract's description of duties.

"I wanted students to feel like they were part of the history, to empathize with colonists," says Waffle. "I think so many times, students don't realize that history is about real people; they think it's more a story, like in a novel." Using primary-source documents helps students "realize that these people actually lived, and ate, and had to survive," she notes. By referring to documents that the colonists actually used, students "walked in the shoes of people who lived there. They were seeing history come alive."

These are the kinds of learning experiences that will stick with students, says Peggy Altoff. "Do we want the Joe Friday approach, a 'just-the-facts-ma'am' recitation?" she asks. "Or do we want kids to think and reason about social studies content?"

The Power of Real-World Experiences

As rhetorical as Altoff's questions may be, there's no harm in addressing them directly. Instructional approaches that ask students to think, reason, interpret, present, analyze, and apply lead to optimal learning. Brain research shows that when students make interpretations and support their conclusions with evidence, they are using the "abstracting, patterning, ordering, prioritizing, judging, and connecting skills of their frontal lobe executive functions." The processes of making observations, discriminating patterns and details, and making connections stimulate and interconnect the brain's memory circuitry. Eventually, "new dendrite sprouts will grow and root the new information into the long-term memory storage banks" (Willis, 2006, p. 54).

It's important to keep in mind that "many of our strongest neural networks are formed by actual experience" (Wolfe, 2001, p. 138). Instructional activities that provide such experiences may involve real-world problem solving, extended-learning projects, and simulations and role-plays. Authentic problem solving, according to Wolfe, gives students a chance to propose solutions to challenges or dilemmas they face in their communities. When students address problems that affect them personally, "it also immeasurably enhances students' motivation, sense of efficacy, and self-esteem" (p. 141).

Joann Winkler has found this to be true. One of her class projects starts as a simulation but ends as an opportunity for students to address the real-world problems of hunger and homelessness. The six-week unit begins with the establishment of a classroom business. "Students are paid for completing their homework and doing classroom jobs, and they use that money to rent their desks, pay utilities, and so on. Students open bank accounts and can earn interest on their money," Winkler explains. During the unit, one student will become "homeless" by losing his or her desk, and the other students must find a solution to the situation. "At first, students want to help each other and will say, 'Oh, you can share my home with me,' or 'I'll lend you money.' Eventually, though, that gets old," says Winkler, who wants her students to see the range of challenges presented by the problem of homelessness and to learn that solutions don't come easy.

For the unit's culminating activity, Winkler's students team up with other students and community members to make ceramic bowls, which become the focal point of a fund-raising dinner party. Attendees make a minimum donation of $10 to eat a simple meal of soup and bread provided by local businesses and to receive a student-made bowl, with all proceeds benefiting the homeless. One recent year, students raised $7,000.

This program has proven to Winkler that when students personally address contemporary societal issues, they gain a lasting sense of empowerment. In fact, high school students who have participated in Winkler's project have decided to tackle homelessness by holding a Homeless Vigil each December.

Wolfe (2001) observes that such real-world projects make the curriculum more meaningful to students, although she cautions teachers to make sure that each project is closely tied to learning objectives and that students understand how the project is linked to what they're learning.

Asking students to contrast the past with the present is one way in which Kathleen Waffle helps her students make such a connection. As a follow-up to her unit on Colonial-era tradesmen, for example, Waffle asked her students to interview local business owners about the challenges they face in running a company today and to conduct in-class presentations that compared the realities of the modern work world with those of the past. "It's important that students understand what came before them and the policies that developed as a result," says Waffle. Her students found, for example, that working conditions were much harsher in Colonial times, and they were surprised to learn that children could be hired as apprentices. This knowledge, Waffle notes, gave her students a new appreciation for child labor laws and compulsory education.

Teachers can further tap into students' imaginations by conducting simulations. Although not "real" events, simulations reflect real-world problems or scenarios and feel authentic to students, thus engaging their emotions and encouraging interaction.

"It's all about historical simulations for me," says Jamie Sawatzky, a 7th grade social studies teacher at Rocky Run Middle School in Fairfax County, Virginia. For a unit on World War I, for example, Sawatzky has created a simulation designed to elicit students' empathy with the people who lived through that period. He drapes sheets of butcher paper over desks to create "trenches" and surrounds them with fake barbed wire and bombs; air-raid sirens wail while students, crouched in the trenches, read *All Quiet on the Western Front* by Erich Maria Remarque.

This book is central to another simulation Sawatzky conducts during the unit. He plays the role of a propagandist, hired to turn public opinion against the German Empire. "I tell the students that the Germans are 'bad' people and show them examples of real propaganda used during that time—one pamphlet shows Germans as apes. The students learn to hate Germany," says Sawatzky. Then the students read *All Quiet on the Western Front,* which chronicles the war through the eyes of a young German soldier. As students begin to connect with the characters, "they start to question their assumptions about German citizens."

Simulation is at the heart of Margit McGuire's *Storypath* curriculum, which is based on a model for instruction and curriculum development used in Scotland in the 1960s. Each "episode" in the multilesson units that make up the curriculum describes a scenario in which students become characters who seek to *do* something—establish a community, create a visitors' center for their state, or determine how to best protect the Great Barrier Reef, for example. Because the simulations enable students to connect personally with social studies concepts, students retain what they learn.

McGuire asserts that civic education should be "front and center" in social studies and that it's essential for students to grapple with what it means to be a citizen. Accordingly, each *Storypath* unit has "some critical incident" that helps students understand their obligations to society. In one episode of the *Storypath* program Democracy in Action, for example, different community members (as played by the students) must determine whether they support or oppose the construction of a new shopping mall in their town. The community members then determine how they will make their views known to other individuals. For example, they could write letters to the newspaper, hold community meetings, or hand out flyers (see Figure 3.1). Through activities like these, McGuire observes, students are practicing literacy skills in context and becoming critical thinkers about the social world in which they live: "We want students to ask questions. Democracy works best when questioned."

Authentic Assessments, Deeper Learning

A position statement by the NCSS (2003b) on fair and equitable assessments notes that assessments should "require higher-order thinking,

FIGURE 3.1

Activity for *Storypath* Episode on Democracy in Action

Episode 5, Portfolio 10

Analyzing the Issue
What is the issue?
What is your position on the issue?
What are the main advantages? Write them in the first column.
What are the main disadvantages? Write them in the second column.

Advantages	Disadvantages

We brainstormed ideas for voicing our opinions about the issue. Look at the list below. Add other ideas from the brainstorming. Circle the one you think is best.

Letters to the newspaper
Flyers
Posters
Community meetings
Marches
Radio interviews

Television interviews
Parades
Internet messages
Signs
Billboards

Prepare your persuasive project.

Use the following checklist as a guide for making your persuasive project:

___ The writing or pictures are forceful and engaging.
___ There is a clear position on the issue.
___ Reasons for the position are clear.
___ Care is shown in the making of the persuasive material.

Source: From *Storypath: Democracy in Action,* by M. McGuire, 2005. Copyright © 2005 by Highsmith Inc. Reprinted with permission.

The Storypath *curriculum includes a portfolio that students maintain as they proceed through the unit.*

writing, and connecting social studies school knowledge to applications in the world outside of school." In addition, the NCSS calls for giving students a variety of ways to demonstrate their knowledge and skills, including "portfolios, performance assessments, written reports, research projects," and so on.

According to education consultant Mary McFarland, performance and content standards are ideal tools for creating such meaningful assessments. Teachers can link lessons and activities to the major learning goals of an entire course, or even of the school year. With those goals in mind, teachers can then identify criteria and design assessments that enable them to gauge students' understanding. "The standards are in service to what you really want to accomplish with your students," McFarland maintains. Teachers should ask themselves, What kind of culminating experience will connect to the entire unit? How can I assess and have students assess their performance? What kind of feedback can I give to help students reach their learning goals?

Ideally, assessments should also help students hone the skills they'll need to be competitive in the ever-changing workplace. As Willis (2006) notes, in the near future there will be fewer blue-collar and administrative support jobs; students will need to be able to perform jobs that "computers and robots cannot" (p. 75). Two of the skills that students will need most are *expert thinking*—which involves "recognizing and organizing patterns and relationships and identifying and solving new problems as they arise" (p. 75)—and *complex communication,* which includes "careful listening and observing to elicit, interpret, and convey critical information" (p. 76). Teachers should design instruction and assessments that enable students to practice these essential skills.

Project-Based Learning and Technology's Edge

Osvaldo Rubio teaches 5th grade at Sherman Oaks Community Charter School in San Jose, California. Many of his students are recent immigrants with limited English skills, and many do not have access to computers at home. Sherman Oaks, which offers a Spanish–English bilingual immersion program and a focus on technology, is the right setting for Rubio to help his students overcome language and socioeconomic barriers and prepare for their futures.

"We try to teach in the constructivist way here, and to allow students to take the lead," says Rubio. Project-based learning is a preferred instructional approach at the school. Through projects, he observes, students "learn a lot and remember what they learned—they more readily recall information when it's their own."

The students are also required to communicate their learning through formal presentations. California state standards call for students to be able to speak before different groups of people, Rubio explains. "I really work hard on helping kids present," says Rubio, who tells his students about how he conquered his own fear of public speaking. "I tell the kids that I had to put my fear aside, that speaking publicly is my job, my responsibility," he says. "I tell them that they need to put themselves out there, too. And I give them as many opportunities to do so as possible."

When he taught 4th grade at Sherman Oaks, Rubio and his students carefully planned for their year-end exhibitions on the history of California's missions. Preparation for the exhibitions, which were open to parents and community members, began with the whole class brainstorming a list of questions, including

- Who founded the missions?
- When were they founded, and where?
- What would a typical day at a mission look like?

"It's up to the students to determine what they want to know. Many times, teachers limit kids by telling them what to do and what to research," Rubio observes. He has found that students become more involved when they can make decisions on their own. For that reason, he specifies the parameters for students' projects but lets students choose their own specific roles. When students "decide who will do what job, they learn to recognize and draw upon one another's strengths," Rubio explains.

The 4th grade mission projects were demanding: students had to give a 5- to 10-minute briefing on their assigned mission; create a drawing or a painting of the mission, along with a poster and a physical model of the structure; and create a movie, a slideshow, or a PowerPoint presentation on the mission. (See "Crafting Rubrics for Tech-Based Projects" for ideas on ways for teachers and students to assess technology-based projects.)

The last component is essential. "We need to incorporate technology," says Rubio, who credits a former principal with helping him articulate his rationale: "The principal said that 'for these kids, using technology should be as easy as using the pencil—that's their future.'" Rubio has enthusiastically embraced that perspective. "The technology is so incredible! We need to give students the opportunity to play with it, to learn

Crafting Rubrics for Tech-Based Projects

Mike Barry

Using technology in social studies classrooms can increase student interest, enthusiasm, and learning. Using rubrics for assessment can help teachers improve the quality of the learning experience—and the products that students create—by helping students to begin work with the end in mind. Here are some pointers for developing effective rubrics for tech-based projects.

Keep It Simple
Use the following four rubric categories, allowing three or four components for each.

- **Content:** Outline the content-area information you want for each project.
- **Design:** Explain what "look" you expect—for example, text styles and sizes, colors, or a certain number of pages or slides.
- **Form:** Designate the technology students should use—should they turn in the project on a disk or as a printout? Present it as a slideshow, an audio recording, a document, or a Web page?

with it. . . . Technology is a new basic," he asserts. What's more, students are thrilled when they see what they can produce with PowerPoint, a digital camera, or any other technological tool: "They get excited—and when they're excited, they learn."

Although technology is an important focus in Rubio's lessons, however, content is still king. Through their projects and presentations, students sharpen their expert thinking and complex communication skills. Although technology contributes to that learning, the work is done in the context of a historical exploration.

This should be the goal for any technology use in school, notes professional development designer Diane Jackson in the online course Technology

---

• **Time Frame:** Highlight dates for checkpoints, drafts, and completion.

State the highest possible score for each area and how all four will be combined for a total score. Weight the criteria you'd like to emphasize. If it's primarily a tech project, pump up the possible points for Form. If you're concerned about information and organization, boost the possible points for Content and Time Frame.

Allow students to ask questions and propose changes to the draft of the rubric. Then have them use the rubric to evaluate a sample project. Discuss their assessments and the best ways to achieve a high-quality project.

A rubric gives teachers a solid context to discuss works-in-progress with their students, which helps students work more efficiently and independently. Because rubrics allow an instructor to pass some of the responsibility for monitoring work to students, it increases their confidence and enthusiasm for using technology in the content areas.

Source: From "Working with the End in Mind: Crafting Rubrics for Tech-Based Projects in the Content Areas," by M. Barry, 2001, *Curriculum Technology Quarterly*, Vol. 11, No. 1. Copyright © 2001 by Association for Supervision and Curriculum Development.

in Schools: It's Not Just About Word Processing (2006). Using technology should lead to "deeper understanding through the development of communication skills," she writes, adding that "at the end of the day, using PowerPoint to create a visually pleasing presentation means only that you've created a visually pleasing presentation."

Using presentation software to illustrate ideas, however, "furthers our development as critical thinkers," notes Jackson. Students need to be critical thinkers first and consumers of technology second: "When PowerPoint is replaced by the next generation of presentation software, the critical thinker . . . will look past the bells and whistles and see the technology for what it is: simply another way to express her ideas. To ensure this outcome, educators need to change the technology paradigm—and their comfort zone—from one of knowing how to use specific software to one of choosing the right technology for effective learning" (2006).

Technological resources bring the world into the classroom. Students can communicate with other students who live oceans away; satellite and Internet technology make it possible for students to participate in a real-time, virtual research community; and innovative educators are finding ways to use geographic information systems as a spatial tool to help students analyze Earth's influence on humanity—and vice versa.

In addition to using this abundance of technology, students should be considering its ethical use, suggests Marsha Alibrandi (2001). "There are significant choices to be made with the availability of these technologies," she writes. "Will they be used for the benefit of humanity and the environment? How are they used by those who exploit natural or man-made resources for personal gain? Will enough of the population know how to use the technology to make reasoned choices?" Talking about such issues has "an established place in the social studies curriculum."

Reflections ◆ ◆ ◆

Educators who are passionate about social studies want to share that excitement with their students. Sometimes, however, a school's climate makes it difficult for teachers to bring the social studies curriculum to life in the classroom. In her article "What Constrains Social Studies Teaching?" (2002), Catherine Cornbleth identifies six climates that hinder effective instruction, which she groups into three categories: stifling, chilling, and drought-stricken. Cornbleth describes the characteristics of these conditions and offers suggestions to help educators weather such climates. If you think your school falls into one of these constraining categories, it would be worth your while to read the article and discuss possible next steps with receptive colleagues.

4 Students as Citizens and Activists

Social activism has long been a way of life for Elizabeth Sinclair. Before becoming a teacher, she worked for the American Civil Liberties Union, interviewing incarcerated women about how they had entered the criminal justice system and then creating programs aimed to help them turn their lives around. Sinclair also worked as a health educator at the University of Washington and developed materials to educate women of childbearing age about fetal alcohol syndrome.

Eventually, Sinclair decided that she was working "at the wrong end of the system" and needed to work with younger kids. So she entered the classroom, bringing along her passion for effecting change. She believes that all students, if given the chance, can be change makers. One year, for example, she was confronted by a group of girls who were angered by the marketing text in a book order form. The form included a list of books that boys would probably like but failed to mention any that girls might enjoy. "The girls were shaking with anger," says Sinclair. She asked the girls to determine what they thought the form should say and encouraged them to write the publisher to share their concerns and ideas. The publisher, much to the girls' delight, wrote back indicating that the form would be changed. "We often don't give kids an opportunity to be as capable as they really are," Sinclair observes.

Sinclair is one of a number of educators who believe that social studies can give students the tools they need to better society, suggests Evans (2006): "These are Deweyan experimentalists who . . . advocate a reflective or issues-centered curriculum" (p. 317). A related group includes social reconstructionists, who "cast social studies in schools in a leading role in the transformation of American society" (p. 317). (See "The Social Studies Wars" for a list of competing interest groups in social studies.)

The Social Studies Wars

Ronald W. Evans

A set of competing interest groups is a relatively constant feature of the social studies arena, struggling at different times either to retain control of social studies or to influence its direction.

The first, traditional historians, supports history as the core of social studies and emphasizes content acquisition, chronology, and the textbook as the backbone of the course.

A second camp advocates social studies as social science and includes those who want a larger place for the teaching of the social science disciplines.

A third group are social efficiency educators. This group hopes to create a smoothly controlled and more efficient society by applying standardized techniques from business and industry to schooling.

A fourth group is composed of social meliorists who want to develop students' reflective thinking ability and, thereby, contribute to social improvement.

A fifth and related group is composed of social reconstructionists or critical pedagogues, who cast social studies in schools in a leading role in the transformation of American society.

Source: From "The Social Studies Wars: Now and Then," by R. Evans, 2006, *Social Education*, Vol. 70, No. 5, pp. 317–321. Copyright © 2006 by National Council for the Social Studies. Adapted with permission. *Social Education* is the official journal of National Council for the Social Studies (www.socialstudies.org).

A Brief History

The notion that school should provide students with the skills and dispositions required for civic engagement and activism has percolated throughout U.S. history. In 1916, philosopher John Dewey echoed Horace Mann's belief that sustaining a democratic society should be the ultimate goal of schooling in the United States. In his book *Democracy and Education,* Dewey wrote that many teachers believed effective teaching could be determined by "the pupil's ability to appropriate and reproduce the subject matter in set statements" (1916, p. 227). But, Dewey argued, instruction that required students primarily to memorize and recite information did not help them grow as members of a social community. Instead, Dewey suggested, students should learn how to integrate skills and knowledge into their lives as participating citizens.

That same year, perhaps as a nod to Dewey's convictions, a national committee convened to reform secondary education. Committee members recommended that all 12th grade students take an interdisciplinary course enabling them to study contemporary societal problems and issues. Through the course, called Problems of Democracy (POD), students would hone the skills necessary for them to become thoughtful and engaged citizens. The problems changed each year and were selected according to their "immediate interest to the class and their vital importance to society" (Caron, 2004).

POD fell out of favor in the 1970s, but many educators—including those on the National Council for the Social Studies (NCSS) board of directors—have made every effort to retain an issues-centered focus in social studies. In 1969, for example, the NCSS board approved—and subsequently reapproved in 2001—a position statement meant to support and safeguard academic freedom. Social studies teachers shouldn't shy away from discussing controversial issues, the authors urged: "It is the prime responsibility of the schools to help students assume the responsibilities of democratic citizenship. To do this, education must impart the skills needed for intelligent study and orderly resolution of the problems inherent in a democratic society. Students need to study issues upon which there is disagreement and to practice analyzing problems, gathering and organizing facts, discriminating between facts and opinions, discussing different viewpoints, and drawing tentative conclusions" (National Council for the Social Studies, 2003).

Capitalizing on Current Events

One way for teachers to maintain an issues-centered focus in the classroom, says Jeff Passe, is to seize the *teachable moment*—the "moment of educational opportunity: a time at which a person . . . is likely to be particularly disposed to learn . . . or made aware of something" (Encarta World English Dictionary, 2006). Because national and global current events fall within the scope of social studies, the subject is replete with such teachable moments. "There are children that are so energized by the study of current events and social issues and cultural differences," observes Passe.

Incorporating current events into the school day is something Mary Knightly does regularly. "In the morning, we discuss the *Scholastic* news," she says. This resource and others like it bring the world into the classroom and begin to build students' global awareness, she maintains.

Other strategies include encouraging students to read local and national newspapers' coverage of current events and asking them to take turns leading class discussions on the controversial issues they read about. Teachers could also assign specific topics: if the students are learning about the U.S. Constitution, for example, they could watch a television news broadcast and note when stories deal with citizens' rights, then engage in a class discussion about how these rights are protected in the Constitution.

Be sure to honor students' previous learning, advises Mary McFarland: "Students know a lot already," so if they seem fascinated by a story that has received widespread news coverage, ask them "to brainstorm what they already know about the topic, whether it's citizenship, leadership, peace, or war." This practice also gives teachers a chance to clarify any misconceptions that students might have.

Once students have enjoyed a robust discussion, "get them to take action on what they know and have learned" about the topic, urges McFarland. If it's an election year and the issue is voter registration, have students create and distribute voter guides or volunteer to help people register to vote, for example. "The more students see that what they're learning is useful, the better," McFarland contends. It's important for students to understand that they *do* know things, "and that that knowing makes a difference," she says.

Capitalizing on the teachable moment can lead to rich learning experiences. Still, Passe concedes that in today's climate of accountability, many teachers are hesitant to depart from their scripted textbooks. Some teachers, especially elementary school teachers, may believe that they haven't been given the training they need to address current events in a meaningful way. So although many social issues are relevant to students, they won't be addressed "unless the teacher feels comfortable doing so," says Passe.

Controversial issues in particular are often overlooked "because teachers don't have the knowledge and instruction to address them," agrees education professor Roger Wolff. The political climate, too, places limitations: "In this rather uncertain time, we hesitate to take a risk and fall back into the tried and true: teaching to content and knowledge rather than addressing higher-order thinking skills." But Wolff has hope: some "really fine educators—and not just teachers—have not bowed to the [accountability] pressure." These educators, he observes, understand that "good educational practice and broad learning results in performance."

Some teachers may not have a solid social studies background, but it wouldn't take long, Passe says, to show them how to effectively teach current events (see "A 10-Point Model for Teaching Controversial Issues"). And, he asserts, in addition to professional development, teachers need "administrators and policymakers who are willing to say, 'Yes, this is what you should be doing.' "

Confronting "Isms" and Phobias

If teachers should discuss societal issues with students, then students should be prepared to tackle those issues, according to Elizabeth Sinclair. "I want my students to be change makers in some way," she says. As a result, her lessons often include opportunities for students to take action.

For example, in one lesson titled Understanding Stereotypes (2002), filmed for Annenberg Media's *Social Studies in Action* series, Sinclair asked her 4th and 5th grade students to consider the term *stereotype* from a variety of perspectives. As students discussed how stereotypes have affected their lives and their learning, Sinclair prompted them to look for the belief behind the behavior: "What thoughts cause a person to act in a certain way?"

That lesson was part of a much bigger project, Sinclair explains: "I taught this particular class the year the [Major League Baseball] All-Star

A 10-Point Model for Teaching Controversial Issues

1. Raise the initial question and have students brainstorm all their initial responses. Write them down. Don't discuss them; accept all contributions. Teacher asks only such questions as, "What does that mean?" "Can you say more about that?" "Does anyone else have anything to add to that information?" and (especially for erroneous or extremely one-sided information) "Where did you learn that?" or "Is that a fact or is it someone's opinion?"

2. As soon as undefined vocabulary words, vague concepts, and unanswered questions emerge, begin a separate list of "things to find out more about." These will serve as guidelines for the ongoing research, and some may even develop into separate topics to pursue later.

3. Information-gathering assignment (homework): Have students find out everything they can about the initial question. Tell them to "be prepared to share what you can in your own words." It is all right to read articles or watch the TV news, but the best source of information is interviewing parents, other relatives, or friends. Do not copy down anyone else's words—but it is all right to take notes in your own words.

4. Share again responses to the initial question in a brainstorming session. Again, students must share the information they gathered in their own words. Write down all responses. Teacher can ask the same questions as in item 1, but offers no information and no "answers." Add to the list of "things to find out more about" from item 2.

5. Continue the process of gathering information, sharing information, identifying things to find out more about, and going out to gather still more information for as long as the topic seems interesting. Encourage students to listen to and learn from each other. They can ask each other to explain what a new word means, to elaborate on a concept, to consider new questions, and to state

their source of information. The teacher's role is an active one, facilitating, clarifying, and questioning, but the teacher doesn't impose information.

6. If a concept emerges that sparks much interest or confusion, pose it as a new question about which to seek information. Share and question until a satisfactory base of information has been established. More than one line of questioning can go on at the same time.

7. Periodically, give the children an individual written assignment in class to summarize their thoughts about a particular question. The assignment can be worded as "what you know about X," "things you don't understand about X," "something X makes you think about," or any other way you can find to help crystallize your students' individual thinking about the topic. Sharing these compositions aloud or posting them for all to read helps make all the information public.

8. As individual or group projects emerge, follow up on them. The class may decide to write letters to public figures; one or two children may decide to pursue a challenging research topic to report on to the group; or an outside resource may unexpectedly appear. Be flexible.

9. Let others—parents, your colleagues, the media—know what you are doing. Invite their participation. Encourage dialogue.

10. Let your project end with something either public or permanent—a class presentation to the rest of the school about what they have learned, an article for the school paper or the local newspaper, a class book or individual books for the school library, or class participation in an event. It is important for children to feel that their learning is relevant and can lead to the ability to make a contribution to the larger world.

Source: From "10-Point Model for Teaching Controversial Issues," by S. Jones, 2007. Copyright © 2007 by Morningside Center. Reprinted with permission. Retrieved January 23, 2007, from www.teachablemoment.org/elementary/teaching_controversy.html

Game came to Seattle." She had decided to link African American history ("a subject I've always taught") with baseball. "We looked at the history of Negro League Baseball, which parallels the history of the Civil Rights Movement," says Sinclair. Each student chose a different player to research. During the course of the students' investigations, they were startled to find "not one mention of Negro League Baseball" in one of their books on African American history.

"What should be done?" Sinclair recalls asking her students. They eventually decided that the players were too important to be excluded from the history book, so they wrote letters to the publisher to persuade her to include the Negro League Baseball players in future editions of the book. The assignment, which met standards for persuasive essay writing, empowered students to act on a strongly held conviction, says Sinclair. The project also helped students find meaning in their learning: "When it's real, when students write something that someone will actually read, they are motivated to do a really good job."

The publisher, unfortunately, could not be reached, and the students "got the whole pack of letters back." Still, although the result may have disheartened students, it didn't disillusion them, says Sinclair: "We had a conversation about the experience and decided it was one worth having. Disappointment is a life lesson, too." Students have to know that no matter the potential outcome, "you have to make an effort."

Such perseverance is an invaluable habit of mind, especially when so many societal problems appear to be unremitting: it seems every generation of students must challenge many of the same isms and phobias. Consider this statement from a student named Brian:

> Right now in Davidson Middle School, gay is the universal word. That's gay, he's gay, she's gay, that teacher's gay, this homework assignment's gay, that pencil's gay, that pen's gay, you know . . . you could use it for anything. Sometimes people literally do mean gay, and sometimes people mean gay as in stupid. . . . People kept on calling me fag, especially in P.E., because that's where most of the older people were. They'd lock me out of the locker room when they were changing so that they wouldn't think that I was checking them out or,

you know, like trying to hit on them when they're undressing and stuff like that. (Women's Educational Media, 2003, pp. 11–12)

"Stories like Brian's reverberate throughout the United States," writes Laura Varlas in "Homophobia in the Halls" (2006). "It's unfortunate that in many schools sexuality or perceived sexuality is still fair game for teasing and harassment."

What is also unfortunate, and disturbing, is that "many teachers seem unprepared or unwilling to facilitate the discussion necessary to . . . eliminate the trauma that many . . . students are experiencing in school today" (Gregg & Thompson, 2004, p. 119). "Gay and lesbian issues can be particularly controversial and are often silenced and marginalized in educational contexts."

Social studies teachers can play a key role in helping students embrace diversity in schools and communities, Gregg and Thompson (2004) suggest: "When one talks about culture, people, individual development, identity, and the common good, one should not leave sexual orientation out of the conversation." Indeed, "anti-oppression education and social justice are themes found in the discipline of social studies" (p. 122).

The earlier teachers help their students combat homophobia, the better. "Knowing that these harmful attitudes can begin in the primary grades, I developed a unit to help my 1st graders learn to respect and value each human being, regardless of sexual orientation. I open the unit by focusing on name-calling," writes Pamela Spycher (1999/2000):

We begin by reading the book *Oliver Button Is a Sissy* by Tomie dePaola. Oliver is a little boy who is teased for doing things that are stereotypically "girl things," such as reading, dancing, and playing dress-up. I talk with the children about how Oliver must have felt when he was harassed for doing the things he loved to do and, essentially, for being who he was.

Then I bring out a big paper doll I made to represent Oliver and ask the class to give me examples of names they have been called or have called other kids. Invariably, the words "gay," "fag," "tomboy," and "sissy" come up. Each time a child calls out a name, I tear a little "wound" in Oliver's body. By the third or fourth tear, the children are cringing.

Then we talk about things we could say to patch Oliver up: "You're my friend" or "I like the way you are." Of course, no matter how much patching we do with tape and nice words, the scars are still visible, and this observation leads to a discussion about how name-calling hurts people deep inside.

Now, when we read a new book that addresses differences or discrimination, I often hear a 1st grader say, "That's just how Oliver Button must have felt." And I know my students are learning the power of empathy.

Honoring Multiple Perspectives

To have empathy, students must walk in others' shoes. The ability to understand and appreciate different viewpoints—and to communicate their own perspectives—prepares students to be citizens in an increasingly global community. Teachers can help students develop a deeper respect for diversity by encouraging them to question the assumptions they hold, to play devil's advocate with their own beliefs.

Teachers need to advise students not to "swallow whole" what someone has taught them, asserts Barbara Coloroso (2003), author of many classroom management and parenting books: "I want students to be asking things." When they study the Alamo, for example, students should ask how the citizens of Mexico view that event; when they learn about the War of 1812, they should find out why Laura Secord is considered a heroine in Canada but a traitor in the United States.

James Banks, director of the Center for Multicultural Education at the University of Washington, agrees: "Students must be given opportunities to look at historical events from these different points of view" (Checkley, 1993). For example, in many U.S. classrooms, students learn about the Westward Expansion strictly from the European point of view: moving across the American continent meant freedom and space for the European settlers. That's a valid perspective, according to Banks, but so too is the perspective of American Indians, for whom the Westward

Expansion meant losing their homeland and giving up much of their freedom. And what about the viewpoints of those who were living in Mexico, Alaska, and even Japan at the time? How could a growing population in the West affect their lives?

Banks believes that social studies can help students learn to ask such questions and, in finding answers to them, gain an awareness of the many different ways of being in the world. Students learn that there are many lifestyles, languages, cultures, and points of view that are valid and should be respected.

The ability to ask questions and to truly listen to the responses is another habit of mind that educators are wise to help students hone. Indeed, some psychologists think the capacity to listen is "one of the highest forms of intelligent behavior" (Costa & Kallick, 2000, p. 23). It's not easy, though: true listening requires students to suspend their own values, judgments, opinions, and prejudices while concentrating on what is being said.

Listening to an alternative viewpoint is all the more crucial when students disagree. Agreement isn't necessarily the desired outcome; understanding is. Good listeners better understand the nature of their disagreement and are better equipped to articulate why they disagree (Costa & Kallick, 2000).

What the World Needs Now

Helping students understand and appreciate multiple viewpoints undergirds effective multicultural and global educational approaches. In fact, "perhaps the most common strategy shared by global educators is their attention to students' learning about events and issues through multiple, usually conflicting, perspectives" (Merryfield, 2002, p. 19).

Instilling in students the "habit of seeking out diverse perspectives" is important, as is teaching students to challenge "sweeping generalizations, misinformation, and stereotypes" (Merryfield, 2002, p. 19). Fortunately, technology makes these tasks much easier for teachers today: "Groups of students can discuss issues facing their communities with online pen pals in Japan, Taiwan, Hong Kong, or Singapore, and regularly report back to their classmates on what they are learning" (Merryfield, 2002, p. 20).

It's difficult for students to accept stereotypes when they have established personal relationships with peers in other countries.

"We live in a global community, and children, from an early age, have to understand the social and community aspects of life as well as the global aspects of life," says Eileen Mesmer, who most recently taught kindergarten and 1st grade at the Saltonstall School in Salem, Massachusetts. Mesmer strongly believes that she has a duty to prepare children for later social studies learning and that "the social part" will help build that foundation. She also thinks that using literature is the best way to get things going.

To introduce the concept of community, for example, Mesmer read aloud *Madlenka* by Peter Sis (2000). The story is about a little girl who is about to lose her tooth and wants to tell all the people in her neighborhood the news. "All her neighbors, who come from many different countries, respond to her in their own languages," Mesmer explains. Students learn that "everyone in our community is different, but we all have commonalities." Teachers can extend this lesson by having students create a K-W-L chart showing what they know, what they want to know, and, after hearing the story, what they have learned about each of the countries represented in *Madlenka*. Students can divide into groups to research particular countries and then share their learning in class. See www.petersis.com/content/madlenka_teachers_guide.html for more ideas.

This learning experience segued nicely into Mesmer's next lesson, designed to help students understand that they belong to more than one community. The book Mesmer chose to read was *Me on the Map* by Joan Sweeney, which tells the story of a little girl who is drawing maps—of herself inside her house, of her house on her street, of her street in her town, of her town in her state, and so on. Mesmer was on her way to school when she came up with an idea that would help make the concept even more concrete in her students' minds.

"I stopped at a hardware store and picked up tubing for a refrigerator," Mesmer recalls. "Then, in the classroom, I created a set of concentric circles." Mesmer asked a student to stand in a circle. She then placed a second circle around the first to represent the street; a third circle represented the town, and so on. As a result, she explains, students "could physically see how a person could be in a room in their house while also being in other places at the same time."

Such early learning experiences are essential in preparing students for a lifetime of interaction with people who are different from themselves—whether those people "live down the street or around the world," says Margit McGuire. If students aren't given opportunities early in their lives to examine similarities and differences among people—if they don't explore what it means to be an individual as well as a part of something larger—then "*different* will be interpreted as *bad,* rather than just *other,*" McGuire contends. "In a time when we're dealing with terror and are so suspicious of others, we have to help kids be discerning and look at people as people. We have to help kids become critical thinkers about the social world in which they live." Once equipped with those abilities, students will be prepared to challenge the isms and phobias that threaten equality, peace, and social justice in their schools, communities, and world.

Merryfield concurs, writing that "the development of open-mindedness, anticipation of complexity, and resistance to stereotyping . . . can all prepare the next generation of citizens to embrace multiple loyalties to our communities, nations, and the planet" (2002, p. 20).

Reflections ◆ ◆ ◆

Capitalizing on the teachable moment can lead to rich learning experiences. Need ideas on how to bring current events and issues into the classroom? Check out www.teachablemoment.org. This Web site, a project of Morningside Center for Teaching Social Responsibility, offers teaching tips and lesson plans for K–12 teachers.

It's never too early to make students aware that they have an obligation, as global citizens, to make the world a better place. Have younger students visit *Planet Tolerance* at www.tolerance.org/pt. The stories and games will entertain while teaching children about the struggle for equality and the need to respect differences.

Implications for Professional Development

5

Imagine this scenario: after having left your homeland and spent months on a crowded vessel crossing a tumultuous ocean, your ship has finally dropped anchor off the coast of Virginia. Your family, along with the many other families aboard the ship, must make this new land your home.

This storyline sets the scene for one of Mary Knightly's favorite units of study: the colonization of the Americas. Her students, working in groups of four, will spend the next two days immersed in the immigrant experience. "The students must tell us why they have left their homes and have chosen this place to set up a new country," says Knightly. Using maps she has provided, students "have to decide where they're going to put their colony and explain why they chose that particular location."

When each group makes its presentation, it's obvious to Knightly that the students have taken their roles as early settlers seriously and have truly considered various potential scenarios. When she asks, for example, why a group didn't choose a different area to call home, her students can readily explain their reasoning and defend their original decision.

Students love these kinds of active learning experiences, says Knightly. And she, in turn, loves to provide them because they allow students to delve deeply into a topic and gain "an appreciation for how other people live, and have lived."

All subjects "can be enhanced by that kind of pedagogy," says Kathleen Waffle, who believes that such active experiences make content come alive for students. She used this reasoning when she helped create a series of workshops designed to show California history teachers how to promote historical thinking while also honing literacy skills, particularly for English language learners (see "The Words That Made America Project").

The workshop's focus is a timely one. High-stakes tests in such subjects as reading and math make it difficult—near impossible, in fact—for teachers to provide the kind of meaningful instruction in social studies that Knightly, Waffle, and so many others support. Thus, it's more important than ever to share with teachers strategies for addressing social studies concepts in ways that enhance their students' understanding. Professional development (PD) is central to this effort.

Simulating the Classroom Experience

When I attended PD events 20 years ago, the purpose was to listen to an "expert" on content related to your teaching field give a lecture on his or her technique. Today, you expect to

The Words That Made America Project

Teachers need a way to expand their repertoires of effective instructional tools and expertise in curriculum development, says Kathleen Waffle—especially when time is at a premium and social studies learning is at stake. Teachers who participate in Words That Made America (WTMA)—a program funded by a federal Teaching American History grant—develop those additional tools and expertise. The strategies are especially useful for teachers who work with English language learners and nonstandard-English-speaking students. Some of the instructional and curriculum development strategies introduced in WTMA workshops include

• Engaging in backwards planning according to content standards.

see a much more interactive session where participants dialogue about the new learning, model the new learning, and
are encouraged to set goals to use the new learning in their
classrooms. (Jonker, 2006)

Many effective educators maintain that learning must be relevant to students' lives. Newmann and Wehlage (1993) note that "a lesson gains in
authenticity the more there is a connection to the larger social context
within which students live" (p. 10). Such connections occur when students "use personal experiences as a context for applying knowledge (such
as using conflict resolution techniques in their own school)" (p. 10).

What's good for the gosling is also good for the goose and the gander,
suggests Mary McFarland, who regularly coaches social studies teachers
who want to create lessons that meet not only social studies standards
but also standards for authentic instruction (see "The Five Standards of
Authentic Instruction," p. 60).

- Creating focus questions for whole-course frameworks, units
of study, and individual lessons incorporating primary sources.
- Critically analyzing student work to assess the quality of lessons in eliciting higher-order thinking from students.
- Writing an analytical paragraph or essay using historical data.
- Designing graphic organizers to assist students in text organization and understanding.

Author's note: Waffle's district teamed up with the Alameda
County Office of Education and educators at Mills College (Oakland,
California) and California State University–East Bay to design and
facilitate the workshops for Alameda County teachers. If you'd like
information on how the partnership evolved and tips on how you
can establish a similar learning and working relationship with educators at a college or university near you, contact Avi Black, ACOE
History–Social Science Coordinator, at ablack@acoe.org.

The Five Standards of Authentic Instruction

Fred M. Newmann and Gary G. Wehlage

To define authentic achievement, we rely on three criteria: (1) students construct meaning and produce knowledge, (2) students use disciplined inquiry to construct meaning, and (3) students aim their work toward production of discourse, products, and performances that have value or meaning beyond success in school.

The five standards of authentic instruction are

1. Higher-Order Thinking. Higher-order thinking requires students to manipulate information and ideas in ways that transform their meaning and implications, such as when students combine facts and ideas in order to synthesize, generalize, explain, hypothesize, or arrive at some conclusion or interpretation. Manipulating information and ideas through these processes allows students to solve problems and discover new (for them) meanings and understandings.

2. Depth of Knowledge. Knowledge is deep or thick when it concerns the central ideas of a topic or discipline. For students, knowledge is deep when they make clear distinctions, develop arguments, solve problems, construct explanations, and otherwise work with relatively complex understandings. Depth is produced, in part, by covering fewer topics in systematic and connected ways.

3. Connectedness to the World Beyond the Classroom. Connectedness occurs when students work on a problem or issue that the teacher and students see as connected to their personal experiences or contemporary public situations. They explore these connections in ways that create personal meaning. Students are involved in an effort to influence an audience beyond their classroom; for example, by communicating knowledge to others, advocating solutions to social problems, providing assistance to people, or creating performances or products with utilitarian or aesthetic value.

4. Substantive Conversation. High levels of substantive conversation are indicated by three features: (1) There is considerable interaction about the ideas of a topic and includes indicators of higher-order thinking such as making distinctions, applying ideas, forming generalizations, raising questions, and not just reporting experiences, facts, definitions, or procedures. (2) Sharing of ideas is evident in exchanges that are not completely scripted or controlled—as when participants explain themselves or ask questions in complete sentences and when they respond directly to comments of previous speakers. (3) The dialogue builds coherently on participants' ideas to promote improved collective understanding of a theme or topic.

5. Social Support for Student Achievement. Social support is high in classes when the teacher conveys high expectations for all students, including that it is necessary to take risks and try hard to master challenging academic work, that all members of the class can learn important knowledge and skills, and that a climate of mutual respect among all members of the class contributes to achievement by all. "Mutual respect" means that students with less skill or proficiency in a subject are treated in ways that encourage their efforts and value their contributions.

Source: From "Five Standards of Authentic Instruction," by F. Newmann and G. Wehlage, 1993, *Educational Leadership,* Vol. 50, No. 7, pp. 8–12. Copyright © 1993 by Association for Supervision and Curriculum Development.

In a workshop with Boston-area educators videotaped for Annenberg Media's *Social Studies in Action: A Methodology Workshop* series, for example, McFarland used the cooperative jigsaw strategy to help participants explore the standards of authentic instruction. Each teacher within a small work group was assigned one of the five standards. Each member of this "home group" then met with members from other groups who were assigned the same standard. Each "expert group" examined its respective standard and determined how a lesson might reflect that standard, after which the experts returned to their original groups to teach their colleagues what they had learned. This jigsaw approach met several standards for authentic instruction. As a bonus, teachers who hadn't used the strategy before were able to add one more effective approach to their instructional repertoire, noted McFarland.

The beauty of strategies like the jigsaw is that they place responsibility for learning on students' shoulders; their classmates are relying on them. "Lots of teachers summarize the content for kids. They lecture and the students dutifully copy down their teachers' bullet points," Mark Stout observes. "I always ask, 'Why are you doing your students' work for them?' " As the curriculum coordinator for social studies in Howard County, Maryland, Stout finds that many teachers "are still very reliant on textbooks" and that weaning them from cookie-cutter activities and traditional approaches is not always easy.

Putting Purpose First

Roger Wolff notes that "one of the biggest challenges is to break the paradigm of looking for activities." He observes that one of the more popular areas of the faculty lounge has long been the magazine rack, where teachers flip through instructional magazines and dog-ear the pages that include the "great activity." Unfortunately, says Wolff, such an activity does not always align with standards and learning objectives. A better practice, he contends, is for teachers to first consider the instructional purpose and then determine an approach that will help students achieve that goal.

"The learning activity is where the teacher and students meet, so it's understandable that [the activity] is what takes the attention of educators," says McFarland. That's why, like Wolff, she supports professional development that helps teachers analyze their instructional goals—not just for one lesson, but for an entire unit or even a year. "We call them 'throughlines'—those learning goals that connect units throughout the year," McFarland explains. Once instructional goals are set, teachers can develop engaging and active lessons and activities as well as performance-based assessments that will help them determine the extent to which students understand the content.

One way McFarland likes to introduce this backward-design, teaching-for-understanding model is to ask teachers to review a lesson, have them conduct the lesson in class, and then ask them to reflect on it, relying on student assessments for additional information. "We might start with a piece of literature or a poem" that students have produced, says McFarland. Then, "we work backwards to determine how that product might have fit into a unit—what the unit goals and standards may have been," she explains. Teachers brainstorm what the instruction preceding the lesson might have looked like, and what kinds of learning experiences might follow it. "Working backwards from a real experience makes eminent sense" and demonstrates to teachers that what they do in class is linked to a much broader educational objective, McFarland notes.

Learning from One Another

> I have found that I get the most out of "On-the-Job" opportunities. . . . I'm working with people in my building, in my grade level, and in my department. The opportunities for collaboration are immense. We can share and I don't always feel like I am reinventing the wheel. I also get fresh and exciting ideas. . . . I don't care for "out of district workshops." I have found that they are not always applicable to my situation and that I need more training . . . to implement what I have been taught. (Locke, 2005)

Whether it takes place during a formal workshop or informal teacher planning time, if a conversation centers on enhancing student learning, it's professional development. Job-embedded professional development, in particular, occurs when teachers support one another in implementing new ideas and programs on site.

When a teacher invites a colleague into his classroom to see a strategy in action, for example, he is both sharing what he knows about that strategy and encouraging input from his colleague on how to refine it. When a principal asks faculty to research curriculum and instructional models, such as *History Alive!* or Understanding by Design, and then has them share what they learn with their colleagues during a faculty meeting, she is making time for job-embedded professional development.

It just makes sense for teachers to learn collaboratively while they're at school, according to Linda Lambert, who notes that "it is vital that teachers and staff members understand the linkage between learning with students in the classroom and learning with colleagues" (2003, p. 21). She further observes that "when teachers learn to facilitate faculty dialogue, they become better at facilitating classroom dialogue; when they listen well to colleagues, they pay the same degree of attention to their students; when they reflect aloud with colleagues, they enable students to reflect aloud; and when they expect to discover evidence to inform their own thinking, they begin to expect students to do the same on the path to problem solving and understanding" (p. 21).

Job-embedded professional development happens, quite naturally, when teachers exercise their leadership ability, notes Lambert, professor emeritus at California State University, Hayward. "When teachers are really leading, they're taking charge of their own destiny and not waiting for others to do something for them," Lambert says. In that leadership comes growth. "Leadership is constructive. It's the process of constructing meaning together to improve the lives of students and the organization," she explains. Such leadership "requires opportunities for ongoing dialogues, for one-on-one conversations and coaching."

One type of job-embedded professional development that has caught on with Roger Wolff's graduate students is action research. In a course that Wolff teaches on the subject, he asks students to "assess the state of learning" in their classrooms. "They ask the questions, 'What am I doing, and is it working?' and 'Are there other things that can be done that could result in greater learning?'" says Wolff. His students, he observes, seem to be quite open to allowing the data they collect to guide their practice.

It's important to be able to analyze data—to "step back a few paces and ask, 'What is it that we want to know about what our students are doing?

What data will tell us?'" agrees Lambert. She advises teachers to look for multiple forms of data, not just test scores. "Our inclination has been to use data quantitatively, but qualitative measures are also data," she observes. Lambert also reminds teachers that it's the "inquiry culture"—that readiness to reflect on and analyze what they do—that really offers the promise of improvement. She is heartened to see that "more and more people are approaching research like anthropologists. They ask questions in a more open-ended way and accept additional criteria to identify success."

Tapping In-House Expertise

Many educators today wonder whether traditional teaching methods really enhance student learning and tend to favor instructional methods that address the needs of more students. Likewise, many educators now also question whether time-honored approaches to professional development actually increase teacher learning and tend to support professional development approaches that will engage and inform more teachers. The result is more active and authentic learning for both students and teachers.

This new understanding about how people learn best is coupled with an appreciation for the many sources of expertise that abound in schools. Just as teachers have learned to tap student expertise to help guide their instruction, school leaders are learning to rely on teacher expertise to achieve professional development goals.

"School districts are looking internally to make better use of their own staff's expertise," writes education consultant Robby Champion (2002). "Drawing on inside expertise proves cost-effective and allows staff learning to be ongoing rather than sporadic."

Consider, for example, the experience Kathleen Waffle has with using primary-source documents to deepen students' understanding of and appreciation for people who lived in times past. When she was a teacher, Waffle attended a workshop held in Colonial Williamsburg to learn how to incorporate the etchings and letters "written 250 years ago by real people" into her lessons. Naturally, she would want to show her colleagues—and now her staff—how to plan similar "goose-bumping" experiences for their students. "It's rewarding to be able to share ideas with teachers that they can incorporate the next day," says Waffle.

Many schools today have educators who, like Waffle, have much to share, says Champion, who specializes in improving professional development. "After years of participating in school improvement initiatives, many veteran teachers have accumulated considerable expertise in a range of sophisticated new teaching protocols," she notes. "These inside experts are delighted when their districts recognize and value their experience and knowledge." The many options for tapping teacher expertise include asking them to serve as mentors, to lead study groups, to model effective lessons, or to act as peer coaches.

Justin Zimmerman offered a combination of such services when he was a mentor teacher at Aberdeen Middle School in Aberdeen, Maryland. "First and foremost, my job was to work with new teachers to ensure their success," says Zimmerman. It wasn't long, however, before other teachers turned to Zimmerman for assistance, too. "These veteran teachers would ask me to observe their classes," he recalls. One teacher wanted Zimmerman to note how many questions he would ask, and how many of those questions required students to use higher-order thinking skills. Another teacher asked Zimmerman to model an effective lesson with a good closing activity.

Although he missed the classroom—he had been a middle school social studies teacher for seven years before becoming a mentor—Zimmerman was impressed with his colleagues' desires to learn and improve. "I loved teaching and being around kids," Zimmerman says. "Still, I reasoned that, as a teacher, I could see maybe 150 kids a day. I wondered how I could be accessible to more students, and it occurred to me that if I could help teachers teach better, I'd be helping more kids."

Teaching and Learning with Technology

It certainly would be helping more kids, some experts contend, if teachers could improve how they use technology in the classroom (see "Technology's Manifest Destiny Remains Unfulfilled")—or, more specifically, how they use technology to assist students in attaining learning objectives.

Persistent misconceptions make it difficult for some teachers to think about using technology as just another tool. Some teachers believe that they have to be technological whizzes to select the right tools. Not true,

Technology's Manifest Destiny Remains Unfulfilled

William D. Pflaum

Like many who found that computers transformed the way they worked, learned, and communicated, I believed the bold promises about the benefits of technology in the classroom:

• Student-centered classrooms, where computers tailor instruction to the individual needs of every learner, would replace the teacher-centered classroom.

• Students would no longer be passive recipients of information. Technology would empower them to become active participants in the construction of their own knowledge. With access to the world's ever-expanding pool of knowledge, schoolchildren would pose relevant questions and find their own answers, often in concert with students in distant lands. They would communicate with renowned scientists, writers, historians, and public figures, joining to solve real-world problems. The barriers of the classroom would dissolve. The classroom would become the world.

• Skills would not be neglected. Engaging multimedia programs would adapt to each student's learning style. Boring drills would give way to fast-paced, individualized, high-interest skill development activities. Static textbooks would gather dust, replaced by dynamic, always-up-to-date learning resources.

• Computer technology would also revolutionize the classroom structure. Teachers would learn alongside their students. They would be facilitators of student self-learning, not purveyors of a one-size-fits-all curriculum. Test scores would soar, or tests would disappear altogether, as newly engaged, motivated students acquired skills, problem-solving abilities, and a newfound thirst for knowledge.

That was technology's promise. The reality, so far, has fallen short. Throughout the 1990s and the early years of this decade,

> test scores have barely budged. Textbooks are still far and away the
> major instructional medium. Dropout rates have remained steady.
> Technology's bold promises have been broken.

Source: From *The Technology Fix: The Promise and Reality of Computers in Our Schools*, by
W. D. Pflaum, 2004. Copyright © 2004 by Association for Supervision and Curriculum Development.

assert other educators, including Jamie Sawatzky, author of the online course Teaching Better with Technology (2003).

"Technology remains simply a collection of tools that allows us to live our lives more efficiently," notes Sawatzky. "Modern technology may give us new ways to obtain information, but the Web sites, smart phones, and online social networking aren't inventing any new data—they're just changing how much and how quickly we gather that data and communicate with each other."

Technology is a tool, plain and simple. When deciding how to use technology to complement or supplement lessons, teachers must start by asking themselves, What do I want students to learn, and how will using this tool help them learn it?

It's important that teachers think beyond content-specific objectives. Technology can be a great aid in helping students hone the lifelong skills they need to develop, including the ability to solve problems, to know when they need to know more, and to know how to find the information they need. But because technology is a double-edged sword, often providing access to more information than students know what to do with, students must also become discerning consumers of all they see, hear, and read.

Indeed, media literacy has become a new basic. According to a *TIME* magazine report released in late 2006, students today need to become "smarter" when they encounter new sources of information. "In an age of overflowing information and proliferating media, kids need to rapidly process what's coming at them and distinguish between what's reliable and what isn't," write Wallis and Steptoe in the report.

"Girls and boys need help deciphering the deluge of images and messages they receive from television, movies, magazines, newspapers, radio, the Internet, podcasts, and so on," agrees Catherine Conover (2006). Conover, the assistant managing editor of *New Moon* magazine, adds that in addition to helping young people "critically analyze the barrage of both text- and image-based messages they receive every day," effective media literacy education also encourages students to "use the tools of this information age—including cameras, camcorders, and computers—to create their own messages." See "Exploring Cultures Through Different Lenses" for an activity idea on media literacy.

Exploring Cultures Through Different Lenses

Each issue of *New Moon* magazine includes a Global Village article that highlights the aspects of a particular culture that pertain to girls and women. The January/February 2006 Global Village article looks at how women become involved in politics in Bolivia, a country that elected a woman president. The young author of the article, Andrea Roman, informs readers that in her country, "girls have the same right to go to school as boys, but in some rural areas, they don't go because of local customs and poverty."

Ask your students to think about how a Global Village article would be executed by various media. What would be the focal point of a *Seventeen* magazine article on Bolivia? How would the *New York Times* report the story? What about *Forbes* magazine? Each publication has a different point of view and would spotlight different information. Paying attention to what is left out of an article can lead to an entirely different interpretation of any story.

Source: From "Fighting Fire with Fire," by C. Conover, 2006, *ASCD Express*, Vol. 1, No. 15. Copyright © 2006 by Association for Supervision and Curriculum Development.

Learning to Use Resources Well

Whether students are asked to analyze some aspect of the media or use technology's tools to create their own messages, it is again incumbent upon the teacher to first determine the learning objective and then help students reap the full benefit of the resources brought to the lesson, suggests Mary McFarland.

McFarland gathered with the same Boston educators who had participated in the *Social Studies in Action* series to examine how teachers could secure students' mental engagement using the wide array of resources designed to enhance social studies lessons—from nonfiction text excerpts, literature, and historical photographs to video clips, recorded speeches, and interactive Web sites. "How do we get students to engage with whatever resource we use?" she asked the participants.

In one activity, the teachers worked in groups to analyze a photograph of civil rights activists gathered on the steps of the Lincoln Memorial to hear Martin Luther King Jr. speak. "What do you know about Dr. King?" McFarland asked the teachers. Once they had identified their prior knowledge, McFarland asked them to imagine that they worked for a newspaper and were assigned to write a story about that event. Relying on the photograph for "clues," teachers then wrote a headline and the first two sentences of the story they would file.

McFarland explained that the teachers had just experienced how a strategy used to teach reading—the SQ3R (Survey, Question, Read, Recite, Review)—could also help students interpret a historical photograph. Teachers could extend the lesson by asking students to reflect on what they had experienced (the SQ4R—add Reflect to the action steps). Students could write a poem or compose a song about what the photo conveyed to them, for example.

For another activity, McFarland wanted the teachers to consider how they could use literature to reinforce social studies concepts. She read aloud the story of a mouse named Frederick who declined to help the other mice in his community gather food for the winter. When the community ran out of food in the middle of the season, the mice turned to Frederick in hopes of obtaining his stash of provisions. Instead of cheese, however, Frederick shared poetic images of springtime that helped dispel the gloom of winter and improved the mice community's mental state.

When she finished reading, McFarland asked participants to decide whether or not Frederick was a good citizen, starting by selecting a number on a 5-point scale, with 1 meaning Frederick was worthless to the community and 5 meaning Frederick was a terrific citizen.

It was the teachers' defense of their positions—from those who thought the mouse was an elitist drain on society to those who felt he helped the other mice learn important lessons in diversity and tolerance—that revealed the deeper value of the exercise, McFarland explained. By engaging in a similarly respectful exchange that explores a full range of opinions, students can learn that in a pluralistic society, not all will agree, and that there are many ways to think about an issue.

Reflections ◆ ◆ ◆

What kind of professional development experiences will help teachers more effectively teach social studies? This chapter presented a sampling of ideas on how to approach teacher learning. As the following comment indicates, however, teachers and principals must work more closely with district leaders to align their efforts:

> As a new teacher a few years ago, I worked with a wonderful group of teachers who helped me learn the ropes. There was an amazing dynamic between the members of our team and we were constantly helping each other and learning from each other. What hindered our progress and consumed our time [were] professional development initiatives. Rarely, if ever, did anyone ask us what we needed, everything was prescribed to us. Not once did someone from our Staff Development Department sit in our meetings and evaluate [our] model of job-embedded professional development. What did happen is that we all burned out and became fragmented under the weight of every "new" initiative instituted to make us better teachers. . . . Anyway, it's ironic that I am now a Professional Developer. I'm hoping that I can practice what I preach. (Miller, 2003)

If you're responsible for professional development in your school or district, how can you avoid the situation described in this comment? For ideas on ways to improve professional development, check out Robby Champion's ASCD PD Online course Ask Now, Not Later: How to Evaluate Professional Development (2002). You might also want to also spend some time browsing Champion's Idea Exchange Web forum, which is focused on improving the quality of professional development. To visit the forum, go to www.ascd.org, click the Community link under the Membership tab, and then click on Idea Exchange.

Afterword
Looking Forward

Time goes by so fast. Parents know this. It seems like just yesterday that little Laura was learning to ride a bike; now she's driving the family car.

Things change so quickly. Social studies teachers know this, too. When Justin Zimmerman first began teaching his geography and global issues class, the controversy of the day was acid rain from Canada. Seven years later, when Zimmerman left the classroom for a new job, acid rain "just wasn't a big issue anymore." Such is the difficulty of writing curriculum for a current events class, he notes.

Still, it was current events that kept Zimmerman charged up, and he noticed that many of his students at Magnolia Middle School in Joppa, Maryland, felt the same way. So he made sure that his social studies classes were fun, interesting, and, most important, relevant to his students' lives.

When Zimmerman's class was videotaped for Annenberg Media's *Social Studies in Action* series, his students had already studied how the destruction of the rain forest affected Brazil and the rest of the globe. They had learned about Japan's education system. They had explored Africa's history and considered why so many African countries continue to struggle today. They had been introduced to the European Union and learned how the legacy of World War II factored into its founding. Now the topic was the conflict in the Middle East.

In the lesson, Zimmerman began by asking students if they knew how the Middle East got its name. Students worked in groups to arrive at a reasoned response. One group of students speculated that the region was so named because it lies both near the equator (Middle) and close to Asia (East). Another group supposed, as did Zimmerman, that the area was named the Middle East because it lay smack-dab in the middle of three continents (which three?).

Once students fixed the geography in their minds, they turned to the conflict that seems to define the region. But before discussing the current discord, Zimmerman asked his students to imagine that they had to settle the following family dispute: a father has died and has bequeathed his home to his three children. Which of those three children should inherit the house, and why? As the students deliberated, Zimmerman posed another question: imagine that their school could teach only one subject: reading, writing, or math. Which of these subjects is the most important, and why?

Zimmerman's students brought training in conflict resolution to their debates, so they were predisposed to search for "win-win" solutions for those embroiled in conflict, and they already understood how difficult it can be to arrive at such solutions. In considering Zimmerman's questions, students came to understand the validity of different viewpoints—a 21st century skill, to be sure.

"My number one goal, when I was a 6th grade teacher, was to help students see how they fit into this world," says Zimmerman, who is now the assistant principal at North East Middle School in Cecil County, Maryland. "I wanted to relate social studies concepts to students' lives and make them relevant so that students can be productive members of society when they get older." As Wallis and Steptoe (2006) note, "kids are global citizens now, even in small-town America, and they must learn to act that way."

That students need to know more about the world is one of several recommendations included in a report from the New Commission on the Skills of the American Workforce. The 170-page report, titled *Tough Choices or Tough Times* (National Center on Education and the Economy, 2007), calls for "high-level competence in the traditional academic disciplines" and in "21st century skills," such as global awareness. Other skills essential to students' competitiveness in the modern world include

- Creativity and innovation.
- Facility with the use of ideas and abstractions.
- The self-discipline and organization needed to manage one's work and drive it through to a successful conclusion.
- The ability to function as a member of a team. (p. 14)

According to Zimmerman, many of these 21st century skills can be developed through social studies. It's through social studies, he observes, that students learn about other cultures and uncover their biases and thereby develop respect for other people. It's through social studies that students can examine why someone who calls customer service may be directed to a consultant in India. "Students need to understand why such trends occur," Zimmerman asserts. "Students need to know why jobs are moving to Mexico and other countries, and why people from other countries come to the United States." It's through social studies, he notes, that students discover how different and how much more diverse the United States is today than it was 50 or 100 years ago.

Such flux makes a social studies education that much more essential, Zimmerman maintains: "I think social studies is the subject by which all that learning can be facilitated." And social studies teachers, he adds, bear the responsibility of preparing students for citizenship in a global society.

"Social studies encompasses everything," says Mary Knightly. Teach geography, and students "gain an appreciation for our physical world," she observes. Teach history and anthropology, and students learn "the histories of people, stories that are often stranger than fiction." With the tough choices students will eventually have to make, "it's important to give them a broader view of the world, of cultures, and of the environment," Knightly says.

"There is a quote that talks about the branches of learning," says Jamie Sawatzky. Social studies, he notes, "is not just a branch, it's the whole tree to which the other branches belong."

"We're teaching discrete math and reading," says Peggy Altoff, who strongly advocates a more balanced educational diet. She worries that students "will be woefully unprepared to assume their responsibilities as citizens. We're not asking kids to think about the events of the past and the future; we're not asking them to think about the economic consequences" of the decisions they make. Without subjects like social studies, says Altoff, "I have so much concern for the future of this country."

These are compelling arguments for fully restoring social studies to the curriculum. It's time to convince the powers that be to listen to reason. Where is Horace Mann when you need him?

Web Resources

- **National Council for the Social Studies** (NCSS) (www.social studies.org). Founded in 1921, NCSS has grown to be the largest association in the United States devoted solely to social studies education.
- **Social Studies for Kids** (www.socialstudiesforkids.com). This site include articles, subjects, and links for all subjects of social studies, with a focus on what kids like.
- **Social Studies School Service** (www.socialstudies.com). This service features more than 15,000 books, videocassettes, CD-ROMs, posters and more that can be ordered online.
- *Storypath* (http://fac-staff.seattleu.edu/mmcguire/web/storypath.html). *Storypath* uses the basic components of a story—setting, characters, and plot—to organize the social studies curriculum into meaningful and memorable learning experiences.
- **The *Social Studies in Action* video library** (www.learner.org/channel/libraries/socialstudies/front). Blending content and methodology, the series documents 24 teachers and their students in K–12 classrooms across the country as they actively explore social studies.
- ***Social Studies in Action: A Methodology Workshop, K–5*** (www.learner.org/channel/workshops/socialstudies/front). This eight-part workshop provides a methodology framework for teaching social studies, with a focus on creating effective citizens.
- **Teaching Tolerance** (www.tolerance.org). Founded in 1991 by the Southern Poverty Law Center, Teaching Tolerance provides educators with free educational materials that promote respect for differences and appreciation of diversity in the classroom and beyond.

• **TeachableMoment.Org** (www.teachablemoment.org). This is a project of Morningside Center for Teaching Social Responsibility (formerly Educators for Social Responsibility Metropolitan Area). TeachableMoment.Org aims to encourage critical thinking on issues of the day and foster a positive classroom environment.

• **Gay, Lesbian and Straight Education Network** (GLSEN) (www.glsen.org). For students, parents, and teachers working toward positive change in schools. GLSEN offers state-by-state action resources for ensuring safe schools for all students.

• **Parents, Families and Friends of Lesbians and Gays** (PFLAG) (www.pflag.org). This organization promotes the health and well-being of gay, lesbian, bisexual, and transgender persons and their families and friends through support, to cope with an adverse society; education, to enlighten an ill-informed public; and advocacy, to end discrimination and to secure equal civil rights.

References

Alibrandi, M. (2001). Mapping life and society: Integrating geographic information systems into social studies. *Curriculum Technology Quarterly, 11*(1), 1.

Allen, R. (2003, Winter). Civic virtue in the schools: Engaging a new generation of citizens. *Curriculum Update,* pp. 1–8.

American Youth Policy Forum. (2005). *Restoring the balance between academics and civic engagement in public schools.*

Arizona Geographic Alliance. (2002). The integration of geography and language arts standards. *Why GeoLiteracy?* Tempe, AZ: Arizona Geographic Alliance. Retrieved February 1, 2007, from http://alliance.la.asu.edu/azga

Ask now, not later: How to evaluate professional development [Online course]. (2002). Alexandria, VA: Association for Supervision and Curriculum Development. Available: www.ascd.org

Barry, M. (2001). Working with the end in mind: Crafting rubrics for tech-based projects in the content areas. *Curriculum Technology Quarterly, 11*(1).

Boston, B. (2005). *Restoring the balance between academics and civic engagement in public schools.* Washington, DC: American Youth Policy Forum.

Brown, J. (2004). *Making the most of Understanding by Design.* Alexandria, VA: Association for Supervision and Curriculum Development.

Caron, E. (2004, Fall). The impact of a methods course on teaching practices: Implementing issues-centered teaching in the secondary social studies classroom. *Journal of Social Studies Research.* Retrieved February 2, 2007, from www.findarticles.com/p/articles/mi_qa3823/is_200410/ai_n9457002/pg_1

Cawelti, G. (2006). The side effects of NCLB. *Educational Leadership, 64*(3), 64–68.

Champion, R. (2002, December). What about inside consultants? Making good use of P.D. models to maximize learning. Message posted to http://webboard.ascd.org:8080/~PDIdeas

Checkley, J. (Producer). (1993). *An interview with James Banks* [Video transcript]. Alexandria, VA: Association for Supervision and Curriculum Development.

Coloroso, B. (Presenter). (2003). *Flexible classroom management styles and the student-learning connection* [Audio recording]. ASCD Conference on Teaching and Learning. Alexandria, VA: Association for Supervision and Curriculum Development.

Conover, C. (2006, May 4). Fighting fire with fire. *ASCD Express* [Online newsletter], *1*(15).

Cornbleth, C. (2002). What constrains social studies teaching? *Social Education, 66*(3), 186–191.

Costa, A., & Kallick, B. (2000). *Discovering and exploring habits of mind.* Alexandria, VA: Association for Supervision and Curriculum Development.

Dewey, J. (1916). *Democracy and education.* New York: Macmillan.

Eakin, S. (2000, Summer). Giants of American education: Horace Mann. *Technos Quarterly for Education and Technology.* Retrieved February 1, 2007, from www.findarticles.com/p/articles/mi_m0HKV/is_2_9/ai_65014459/print

Evans, R. (2006). The social studies wars: Now and then. *Social Education, 70*(5), 317–321.

Gregg, L., & Thompson, S. (2004). Beyond tolerance: A place for acceptance of gay, lesbian, bisexual, and transgendered people in our schools. In S. Adler (Ed.), *Critical issues in social studies teacher education* (pp. 117–130). Greenwich, CT: Information Age Publishing.

Guilfoyle, C. (2006). NCLB: Is there life beyond testing? *Educational Leadership, 64*(3), 8–13.

Haskvitz, A. (2006, March 22). The disrespecting of social studies. *EdNews.org* [Online newsletter]. Retrieved February 1, 2007, from www.ednews.org/articles/547/1/The-Disrespecting-of-Social-Studies/Page1.html

Jonker, D. (2006, November 6). Lesson 1 discussion question. Message posted to http://webboard.ascd.org:8080/~asknow

Lambert, L. (2003). *Leadership capacity for lasting school improvement.* Alexandria, VA: Association for Supervision and Curriculum Development.

Locke, J. (2005, March 7). Lesson 1. Message posted to http://webboard.ascd.org:8080/~asknow

McGuire, M. (2005). *Storypath: Democracy in action.* Fort Atkinson, WI: Highsmith, Inc.

Merryfield, M. (2002). The difference a global educator can make. *Educational Leadership, 60*(2), 18–21.

Miller, T. (2003, January 2). Discussion question. Message posted to http://webboard.ascd.org:8080/~asknow

National Center on Education and the Economy. (2007). *Tough choices or tough times: The report of the New Commission on the Skills of the American Workforce.* San Francisco: Jossey-Bass.

National Council for the Social Studies. (2003a). *Academic freedom and the social studies teacher. NCSS position statements.* Retrieved February 2, 2007, from www.socialstudies.org/positions/freedom

National Council for the Social Studies. (2003b). *Promoting fair and equitable assessments. NCSS position statements.* Retrieved February 2, 2007, from www.socialstudies.org/positions/assessment

Newmann, F., & Wehlage, G. (1993). Five standards of authentic instruction. *Educational Leadership, 50*(7), 8–12.

Pflaum, W. D. (2004). *The technology fix: The promise and reality of computers in our schools.* Alexandria, VA: Association for Supervision and Curriculum Development.

Popham, W. J. (2006). Curriculum standards: The unindicted co-conspirator. *Educational Leadership, 64*(1), 87–88.

Scherer, M. (2006). Perspectives: The NCLB issue. *Educational Leadership, 64*(3), 7.

Seif, E. (2003/2004). Social studies revived. *Educational Leadership, 61*(4), 54–59.

Social studies in action: Understanding stereotypes [Online course]. (2002). Washington, DC: Annenberg Media. Available: www.learner.org/channel/libraries/socialstudies/3_5/sinclair

Spycher, P. (1999/2000). Sticks and stones: Teaching the power of empathy to young children. *Classroom Leadership, 3*(4).

The Task Force of the National Council for the Social Studies. (1994). *Expectations of excellence: Curriculum standards for social studies.* Silver Spring, MD: National Council for the Social Studies.

Teaching better with technology [Online course]. (2003). Alexandria, VA: Association for Supervision and Curriculum Development. Available: www.ascd.org

Technology in schools: It's not just about word processing [Online course]. (2006). Alexandria, VA: Association for Supervision and Curriculum Development. Available: www.ascd.org

Varlas, L. (2004, Summer). Viewpoint: An interview with Denee Mattioli. *Curriculum Technology Quarterly.*

Varlas, L. (2006, November 30). Homophobia in the halls. *ASCD Express* [Online newsletter], 2(4).

Wallis, C., & Steptoe, S. (2006, December 10). How to bring our schools out of the 20th century. *TIME.* Retrieved February 2, 2007, from www.time.com/time/magazine/article/0,9171,1568480,00.html

WGBH Educational Foundation. (2003). *Social studies in action: A methodology workshop, K–5. Workshop 4: Applying themes and disciplines.* Washington, DC: Annenberg Media.

Willis, J. (2006). *Research-based strategies to ignite student learning.* Alexandria, VA: Association for Supervision and Curriculum Development.

Wolfe, P. (2001). *Brain matters: Translating research into classroom practice.* Alexandria, VA: Association for Supervision and Curriculum Development.

Women's Educational Media. (2003). *Let's get real: Final transcript.* San Francisco: Author. Available: www.womedia.org/lgr_transcript.pdf

Index

Note: page references followed by *f* refer to figures.

Related ASCD Resources: Social Studies

Print Products

Curriculum Technology Quarterly, Summer 2004: Technology for the Social Studies Classroom (#104019)

Education Update, May 2006: "Social Studies Jockeys for Position in a Narrowing Curriculum: NCLB a Thief of Time" (#106018)

Educational Leadership, September 2004: Teaching for Meaning (#105028)

Educational Leadership, December 2003/January 2004: New Needs, New Curriculum (#104026)

Educational Leadership, October 2002: The World in the Classroom (#102306)

Social Studies: A Curriculum Handbook, Spring 2003 (#103002)

Talk It Out: Conflict Resolution in the Elementary Classroom by Barbara Porro (#196018)

Teaching Reading in Social Studies: A Supplement to Teaching Reading in the Content Areas Teacher's Manual by Jane K. Doty, Gregory N. Cameron, and Mary Lee Barton (#303357)

Videos and DVD

The Lesson Collection Tape 36 Social Studies (Categorizing) (Intermediate School) (#403352)

The Lesson Collection Tape 38 Social Studies (Articles of Confederation) (Middle School) (#403354)

The Lesson Collection Tape 43 Social Studies (Native Americans) (Intermediate) (#404460)

For more information, visit us on the World Wide Web (www.ascd.org); send an e-mail message to member@ascd.org; call the ASCD Service Center (1-800-933-ASCD or 703-578-9600, then press 2); send a fax to 703-575-5400; or write to Information Services, ASCD, 1703 N. Beauregard St., Alexandria, VA 22311-1714 USA.